PROPHECY · PHENOMENA · HOPE

BOOKS BY ROBERT POWELL

Christian Hermetic Astrology
The Star of the Magi and the Life of Christ

Chronicle of the Living Christ
The Life and Ministry of Jesus Christ
Foundations of Cosmic Christianity

Elijah Come Again
A Prophet for Our Time
A Scientific Approach to Reincarnation

The Most Holy Trinosophia
The New Revelation of the Divine Feminine

The Mystery, Biography & Destiny of Mary Magdalene
Sister of Lazarus John & Spiritual Sister of Jesus

The Sophia Teachings
The Emergence of the Divine Feminine in Our Time

BOOKS COAUTHORED WITH KEVIN DANN

The Astrological Revolution
Unveiling the Science of the Stars
as a Science of Reincarnation and Karma

Christ & the Maya Calendar
2012 & the Coming of the Antichrist

EDITED BY ROBERT POWELL

Journal for Star Wisdom (annual)

The Clockwise House System
A True Foundation for Sidereal and Tropical Astrology
by Jacques Dorsan (edited with Wain Farrants)

PROPHECY
PHENOMENA
HOPE

The Real Meaning of 2012

Christ & the Maya Calendar
An Update

ROBERT POWELL

Lindisfarne Books
2011

LINDISFARNE BOOKS
An imprint of SteinerBooks / Anthroposophic Press, Inc.
610 Main St., Great Barrington, MA 01230
www.steinerbooks.org

A NOTE ABOUT THE TERM *ANTICHRIST*

The word *Antichrist* is used throughout this book, and there are at least
two ways in which this word may be understood. The more general use
of the word is found in the Bible and in Christian tradition, in which the
Antichrist is understood to be the human being who bears the incarnated
Satan (also called "Ahriman" in Persian tradition and, in Revelation
13, "The Beast"). This is how the word *Antichrist* is used in this book.
However, this general meaning should be distinguished from another, more
specialized use of the word, as found in Rudolf Steiner's Anthroposophy,
in which the word *Antichrist* frequently refers to the Sun Demon, known
as Sorath in the Hebrew tradition and referred to as the "Beast whose
number is 666," and as "the two-horned Beast" in Revelation 13. In this
connection, Rudolf Steiner refers to "the False Prophet who represents the
teachings of The Beast." See the table on page 31.

Print edition: ISBN 978-1-58420-111-3

eBook edition: ISBN 978-1-58420-110-6

CONTENTS

INTRODUCTION

The prophecy that is most central to this book points toward the very real potential of the phenomenon of possession being played out on the world stage. This phenomenon and other phenomena associated with it call for an awakening of world consciousness and, above all, world conscience on the part of all humanity.

This book is an update on the book *Christ & the Maya Calendar* (2009), seeking to shed light on the phenomena of our time through the lens of Christian tradition and the prophecies of Rudolf Steiner. This book, *Prophecy • Phenomena • Hope*, examines, together with Steiner's prophetic indications, a prophecy coming from American soil through Jeane Dixon, as well as the prophecies from Russian sophiology through Vladimir Solovyov and Daniel Andreev. Also considered here is a finding from the spiritual research of the young anthroposophist and stigmatist Judith von Halle.

All of this is to say, by way of introduction, that this offering is strongly Christian in tone. In the more universal, esoteric understanding that Christ is a cosmic reality, this research is intended to serve as an awakening call to be vigilant in face of the phenomena now playing out on the world stage—i.e. to look carefully and observantly at what is now steadily unfolding before our eyes...connecting the dots in relation to what is spelled out by current events.

LOOKING THROUGH THE HEART OF DARKNESS INTO THE LIGHT

In 2009, the book *Christ & the Maya Calendar: 2012 and the Coming of the Antichrist* was published. It gives some background to what Rudolf Steiner referred to as "a spiritual struggle to which nothing in history is comparable,"[1] and for which we have to be spiritually prepared. According to the research presented in this book, we are fast approaching "the day when evil comes" (Ephesians 6:13). Because of the investigative nature of the book, since its publication

---

1   Steiner, *Freemasonry and Ritual Work*, p. 449.

by Kevin Dann and myself, some readers have raised the question whether the central prognosis outlined in the book has been/is being/will be fulfilled—and, in the latter case, whether it will be fulfilled in the near future? Readers may question why one should devote any attention to a prophecy of such a dark nature. Why not simply focus on the Good, the True, and the Beautiful?

An answer to this question is offered by Judith von Halle, who underwent a life-transforming experience on Good Friday in 2004, when she received the stigmata, the visible manifestation of the wounds of Christ:

> Striking utterances by Steiner about the mystery of the reappearance of the etheric Christ and the impulse of His adversary, the anti-Christ, in the twentieth and twenty-first centuries, are only seldom examined, illumined, or cited.... In perception of and engagement with this highly topical phenomenon of our times, a scarcely explicable kind of paralysis seems to have taken hold of human spirits. There seems no other way to explain this paralysis than as the latent effect of the power of the anti-Christ himself. If one begins to speak of this theme, even tentatively, the reactions one receives—from anxiety through to fairly inexplicable, outright rejection—show how people unconsciously experience and perceive this power as very present and real.... [The] first task is to devote [oneself] entirely to the Christ Mystery with all [one's] thinking, feeling, and will. This Christ Mystery, however, inevitably encompasses the Mystery of His adversary. The esoteric pupil could not learn to grasp the deeds of Christ—both those at the turning point of time and those of the contemporary Christ being today—and could never develop a fuller understanding of the Christ being and His significance for future human evolution, let alone find the path to redemption...[without] also enquir[ing] into all that seeks to prevent [one] from following [the] Redeemer.[2]

Prophecy · Phenomena · Hope focuses on the two themes to which Judith von Halle refers: the reappearance of Christ (his Second Coming) and the increasing influence of Christ's adversaries upon humanity and the Earth, prophesied to attain a certain culmination with the

---

2   Von Halle, *Descent into the Depths of the Earth*, pp. 49–50.

incarnation of Ahriman. In reading this book, it is important to bear in mind that Rudolf Steiner forewarned of a possible catastrophe for humanity if the incarnation of Ahriman, which he prophesied to take place shortly after the year 2000,[3] were to go unrecognized. The implication is that, because of a lack of awareness on the part of human beings, the possibility exists that this incarnation might go unnoticed, in which case, according to Rudolf Steiner, a great opportunity for humankind's spiritual evolution would pass by, leading to very serious consequences for humanity and the Earth. This leads us to consider the possibility that *the reason for this dark event is to serve as a spiritual awakening for humanity. How may this be understood?*

The time in which we are presently living is known as the *age of the consciousness soul.*[4] It is during this time that the Mystery of Evil is being unveiled, just as in the previous age the Mystery of Death was the primary theme.[5] In the previous epoch (747 BC–AD 1414), known

---

3   Ahriman is the ancient Persian/Zoroastrian designation for the prince of darkness, known as Satan in the Judeo-Christian tradition. Rudolf Steiner preferred to use the name Ahriman. It should be noted that in the Christian tradition, the event referred to by Rudolf Steiner as the *incarnation of Ahriman* is designated as the coming of the Antichrist. In the words of Rudolf Steiner: "Before only a part of the third millennium of the post-Christian era has elapsed, there will be in the West an actual incarnation of Ahriman— Ahriman in the flesh." This prophetic statement relating to now was made in a lecture held on November 1, 1919 (see Steiner, *The Incarnation of Ahriman*, p. 37). It should be noted, further, that Rudolf Steiner and Judith von Halle use the word *Antichrist* not to designate the incarnation of Ahriman, but to describe the Sun demon known as Sorath, whose number (in Hebrew) is 666 (see Revelation, chapter 13). See also the table on page 31.

4   In Rudolf Steiner's description of spiritual evolution, successive periods of 2,160 years corresponding to the signs of the zodiac unfold historically. He called these periods cultural epochs. He described the age of the consciousness soul as the fifth cultural epoch since the destruction of Atlantis through the great flood and dated this current fifth epoch, corresponding to the Age of Pisces, from the year 1413/1414 to 3573/3574. As described in Powell & Dann, *The Astrological Revolution*, the Age of Pisces lasts 2,160 years and extends from AD 215 to 2375, and the corresponding cultural epoch, the age of the consciousness soul, began in 1414—after a time-lag of 1,199 years – almost twelve hundred years after the start of the Age of Pisces, where the time-lag of 1,199 years is an astronomical period associated with the planet Venus, comprising two 600-year cultural waves. According to Rudolf Steiner, a cultural wave lasts for six hundred years, whereas a cultural epoch lasts for 2,160 years.

5   Steiner, *Freemasonry and Ritual Work.*

as the age of the mind (or intellectual) soul, the Mystery of Death was "solved" by Christ's resurrection—overcoming death. Now, in our time, this book is written to encourage a connection with the *Parousia,* the presence of Christ in the etheric, the weaving life forces of the Earth, as a protective mantle and guiding light during these times and the times ahead, when the Mystery of Evil is becoming unveiled.

The purpose of unveiling evil in our time is to awaken consciousness. Both Good and Evil exist. Both are aspects of world existence. Awaking to Good and awaking to Evil go hand in hand. Mystics have sometimes described how the gates of heaven and hell open simultaneously. The higher self ("I") of the human being is able to behold the Mystery of the Good, while at the same time the lower "I" perceives the Mystery of Evil. A spiritual awakening such as that exemplified by Rudolf Steiner signifies beholding with the higher "I" and with the lower "I" simultaneously. In this case, a high degree of spiritual wakefulness is active. It could be added that it is through the strength of the light of beholding the Etheric Christ[6] that one will be able to bear the beholding of the incarnation of Ahriman. The emergence of the *Antilogos* (to use Daniel Andreev's expression)[7] is the shadow side of awakening to the *Parousia,* the Presence of Christ in the etheric realm, and cognition of both, as exemplified by Rudolf Steiner, is possible through the beholding of the higher "I" and the lower "I" working together.

By way of analogy, let us consider the Mystery of Golgotha—extending over three days and comprising the crucifixion (Good Friday), the descent into the depths of the Earth (Holy Saturday), and the resurrection (Easter Sunday)—at the culmination of Christ's coming in a physical body two thousand years ago. Here, too, the Mystery of Evil played a role. This manifested, in particular, in an ahrimanic impulse taking possession of one of Christ's disciples, Judas Iscariot, who then betrayed his Master. What is meant here by an ahrimanic impulse?

It has to do with Ahriman's influence upon the human being in "hardening the heart." Thus, for example, when the driving forces

---

6   See my article "The Mystery of Christ in our Time" for further elucidation concerning the Etheric Christ as the *Parousia, the Presence of Christ in the etheric realm in our time:* https://sophiafoundation.org/articles/.

7   *Journal for Star Wisdom 2011,* p. 13; see also appendix 1.

toward power and money gain the upper hand, the discerning forces of the human heart become hardened and the guiding impulses of the higher "I"—the perceiver and knower of the Good in the world and in the human being—are to a greater or lesser extent occluded, unable to shine into human consciousness.

Bearing witness to the wisdom inherent in the practice of beholding with the higher "I" and the lower "I" simultaneously, paradoxically it was this very betrayal that enabled Christ's sacrifice at the Mystery of Golgotha two thousand years ago to take place. Now, in our time, it is possible that the Judas role is to be played by a personality on the world stage, a human being of whom Ahriman will take possession, thus betraying the Etheric Christ, betraying the entire etheric realm of nature in which the Etheric Christ is active, and betraying humanity. Considering the state of the world today, could it be that this betrayal is now upon us?

At the Last Supper, Christ spoke the words to Judas: "What you are about to do, do quickly!" (John 13:27). An encroaching mood of aggressive activity is now accelerating and resounding in the Earth's spiritual environment. Might this signal the approach of the incarnation of Ahriman? Paradoxically, it will be a betrayal of this magnitude—a movement toward anti-life on a global scale—that sets the stage for the fulfillment by the Etheric Christ of a sacrifice comparable to that at the Mystery of Golgotha, a sacrifice of cosmic dimension to realign the Earth with the heavens. Not unlike the disciples falling asleep in the garden of Gethsemane, humankind, in the approach of this great sacrifice, is—by and large—asleep to it and to the drama that is currently unfolding.

The endeavor of this short book is to serve as a wake-up call, as was—and still is—also the purpose of the book *Christ & the Maya Calendar*.

KARMIC BACKGROUND OF A POTENTIAL HUMAN VESSEL

Following upon the prophetic visions of the American seer, Jeane Dixon, together with those formulated by the great Russian seer, Daniel Andreev, one can consider three hypotheses:

a) formulated by Daniel Andreev in his book *The Rose of the World* (completed in 1958) that "Mr. X ," the individuality who has been chosen to serve as the human vessel for Ahriman's incarnation, will be the reincarnated individuality of Joseph Stalin.

b) formulated by Jeane Dixon in her book *My Life and Prophecies* (published in 1969) that Mr. X was born on February 5, 1962.

Taking (a) and (b) together leads to a third hypothesis,

c) that the reincarnated Joseph Stalin was born as Mr. X, on February 5, 1962, and that, consequently, February 5, 2012, is the fiftieth birthday of this individual.

It is important to bear in mind that (a), (b), and (c) signify a series of hypotheses. Following the scientific approach of Astrosophy, how might we proceed further in this line of inquiry? Ultimately, the ideal way of testing is through our sense for truth and our ability to discern on a deeper level. Time will tell, as in the course of time all will be revealed, in the spirit of Christ's words: "By their fruits you shall know them" (Matthew 7:16). Meanwhile, it is possible to test (c) astrosophically. To do this, we can compare the horoscope of Stalin's death with the horoscope of the February 5, 1962 birth of Mr. X as indicated in Jeane Dixon's vision.

Against this background, the purpose of this book is to create a framework in which the reader is able to come to recognize the signature of this individuality, a telling sign, to help facilitate a recognition which is, according to Rudolf Steiner, of such vital significance for the evolution of the Earth and humanity. What to do, then, with this cognition? This requires an activity of choice, a constancy of choosing life over anti-life, focusing upon the all-abiding presence of Divine Love as the ultimate source of all that exists.

As indicated by Judith von Halle, quoted on page 8: "[The] first task is to devote [oneself] entirely to the Christ Mystery with all [one's] thinking, feeling, and will." It is a matter of placing the Etheric

Christ in the foreground, and always seeing the adversarial forces against this foreground. A schooling of a stream of inner radiance through connecting with the Etheric Christ by way of the etheric form of movement known as eurythmy is now possible. The expression of Christ's words in conjunction with this etheric form of movement (eurythmy) offers a path to the Etheric Christ and protection against the adversarial forces, bearing in mind that "Heaven and Earth will pass away, but my words will never pass away" (Matthew 24:35).[8]

Moreover, as described in chapter 2 of *Christ & the Maya Calendar*, according to the Apocalypse Code, there are still some 36,000 years of evolution until the end of the Earth period, during which Christ—who said, "I am with you always until the end of time" (Matthew 28:20)—is ever-present as guide and companion, blessing all human beings who align themselves with him. Against this background, the coming of the Antichrist (the incarnation of Ahriman) as described in Revelation, chapter 13, is only a passing, temporary phase in relation to the great sweep of Earth evolution lying ahead, portrayed archetypically, as meta-history, in chapters 14 to 22 of Revelation.

THE UNVEILING OF A VENUS MYSTERY

Returning now to look at the comparison horoscope between Stalin's death and the birth of the potential candidate for Mr. X, we shall consider the comparison of the two charts heliocentrically. The reason for this is that, from the heliocentric horoscope comparison, it is possible to see if recurring astrological rhythms that signal an indication of reincarnation patterns are evident. These rhythms are described in my books *The Astrological Revolution* and *Elijah Come Again*.[9] Without going into too much detail here, a quick glance shows the first pattern, having to do with the angular relationship between the Sun and Saturn; in the heliocentric horoscope this is equivalent to the angular relationship between the Earth and Saturn,

---

8   Powell, *The Morning Meditation in Eurythmy*, gives instruction in schooling the stream of inner radiance by connecting with the Etheric Christ through the etheric form of movement known as eurythmy. See also footnote 34.

9   Powell, *Elijah Come Again*; Powell & Dann, *The Astrological Revolution*.

Comparison Chart

Outer - Heliocentric	Inner - Heliocentric
Death of Joseph Stalin	Birth of Antichrist (V. 1)
At Moscow, Russia, Latitude 55N45', Longitude 37E36'	At Tobruk, Latitude 32N6', Longitude 23E56'
Date: Thursday, 5/MAR/1953, Gregorian	Date: Monday, 5/FEB/1962, Gregorian
Time: 21:50, Time Zone EET	Time: 7:20, Time Zone EET
Sidereal Time 9:13:25, Vernal Point 5 ✕ 54'49"	Sidereal Time 15:55:32, Vernal Point 5 ✕ 47'21"

Zodiac: Sidereal SVP
Aspect set: Conjunction/Square/Opposition

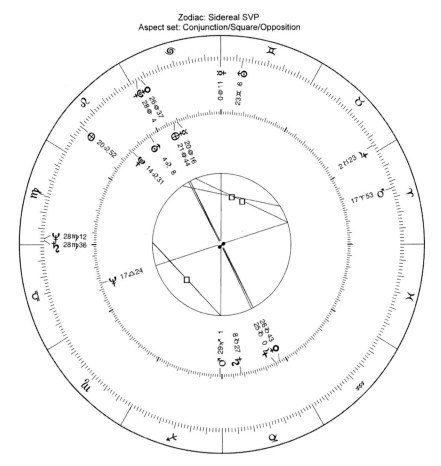

which in this example is not fulfilled. However, the second pattern, having to do with significant reoccurring alignments, is fulfilled in a very precise way. The second "rule", or reoccurring pattern, concerns the alignment heliocentrically from death in one incarnation to birth in the next incarnation of Mercury and/or Venus. In this case heliocentric Venus at Stalin's death was located at 26½ degrees Cancer (see outer circle of comparison horoscope) and heliocentric Venus at the birth of Mr. X was located exactly opposite at 26½ degrees Capricorn (see inner circle of comparison horoscope).

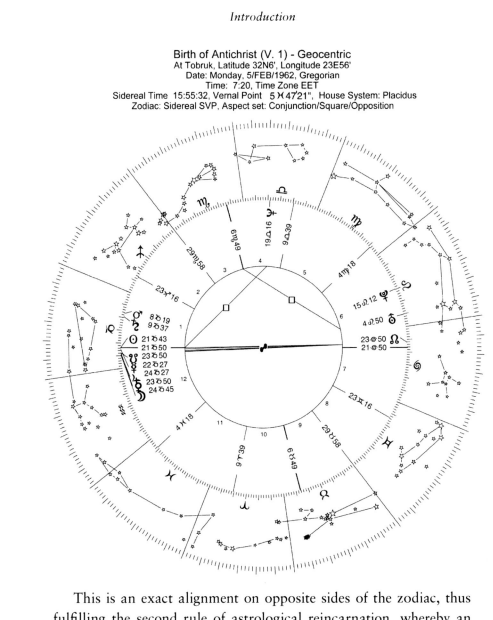

Birth of Antichrist (V. 1) - Geocentric
At Tobruk, Latitude 32N6', Longitude 23E56'
Date: Monday, 5/FEB/1962, Gregorian
Time: 7:20, Time Zone EET
Sidereal Time 15:55:32, Vernal Point 5 ♓47'21", House System: Placidus
Zodiac: Sidereal SVP, Aspect set: Conjunction/Square/Opposition

This is an exact alignment on opposite sides of the zodiac, thus fulfilling the second rule of astrological reincarnation, whereby an alignment occuring either on the same side of the zodiac or on opposite sides of the zodiac points toward an indication of a "seeding" impulse coming to fulfillment in the next incarnation. In addition to the heliocentric Venus alignment, there are several other striking alignments of planets on opposite sides of the zodiac; one could liken this to a New Moon/Full Moon perspective. Without going into detail about these alignments, which would require a more comprehensive book, it is possible to say that these alignments may indicate rhythms of continuity of purpose from one incarnation to the next. See the following tabulation for alignments:

Heliocentric planetary positions in the sidereal zodiac at the death of Joseph Stalin	Heliocentric planetary positions on the opposite side of the sidereal zodiac at the birth of Mr. X
Venus at 26°37' Cancer	Venus at 26°43' Capricorn
Venus at 26°37' Cancer	Jupiter at 25°00' Capricorn
Mercury at 0°11' Cancer	Mars at 29°01' Sagittarius
Mars at 17°53' Aries	Neptune at 17°24' Libra
Pluto at 28°04' Cancer	Venus at 26°43' Capricorn

With this exact fulfillment of the second rule of astrological reincarnation, and the occurrence of several other alignments, astrosophical evidence is provided in support of the feasibility of hypothesis (c). While this does not prove hypothesis (c), it lends support to it. Perhaps a way to see this is that there were forces at work within the soul of Stalin that we can recognize as active on the world scene today.

Note that, in the horoscope, the *place* taken for the birth is Tobruk, Libya. This follows Willi Sucher's indication (see bibliography) concerning the birthplace of the vessel (Mr. X). The time taken for the moment of birth: sunrise, exactly as the Sun was rising, was indicated by Jeane Dixon. Research reveals that the birth of Mr. X at sunrise on February 5, 1962, in Tobruk, Libya, would have taken place only five hours after a total eclipse of the Sun in the sidereal sign of Capricorn. Simultaneously, on that day there was a most spectacular alignment of planets in Capricorn—as indicated by Jeane Dixon—with Saturn, Jupiter, Mars, Venus, the Sun, Mercury, and the Moon aligned with the Moon's Node in Capricorn. The last time a grand conjunction of the seven visible planets occurred was in 1524. Historically, the year 1524 marked the beginning of the Age of Gabriel (1524–1879), the age that preceded the present Age of Michael (1879–2234). If the future "world president" was actually born on this date in 1962, then he was born with the most powerful horoscope imaginable—an *imperial horoscope,* to use the terminology of Roman astrologers casting horoscopes for members of the emperor's family. These astrologers ascribed imperial power to horoscopes of those born with two or more planets in proximity to the Ascendant. In the 1962 horoscope, all seven classical planets are close to the Ascendant (see geocentric birth horoscope on page 15). If the chosen candidate for the vessel for Ahriman's incarnation was indeed born on February 5, 1962, then in 2011 he turned forty-nine years of age, signifying an important time in the unfolding of his destiny—a time having to do with the start of a new seven-year cycle, the Jupiter cycle in his life, which is generally reckoned to be the peak seven years of life (49 to 56) in terms of power and influence in the world.[10]

In Rudolf Steiner's series of lectures entitled *Karmic Relationships,* held during 1924, shortly before his death in 1925, it emerges (not explicitly, but implicitly) that he was speaking on behalf of the Archangel Michael, revealing something of the Divine Plan. He addressed his listeners as members of the "school of Michael," as human beings coming under the aegis of Michael to act in this Archangel's service from incarnation to incarnation on Earth. Since Michael is the "right hand" of Christ, as the leader of the heavenly hosts in the great battle with Ahriman and the anti-Christian forces allied with Ahriman, these human beings can also be considered servants of Christ. Rudolf Steiner pointed out that the school of Michael comprises a vast community of human beings and spiritual beings concerned with fulfilling the Divine Plan as servants of Michael and Christ. And since the Divine Plan is embodied by Sophia, the divine matrix for the wisdom of creation, one could also add the name Sophia here. Given this background, it is plausible to contemplate the possibility that human beings who are attracted to the work of Rudolf Steiner belong, by and large, to the school of Michael, whose motto could be formulated: "Michael and Sophia in the name of Christ."[11]

Thus the question is raised: What can we do in face of the unveiling of the Mystery of Evil as we perceive it in our world today—evil at

---

10   For further background concerning the birth horoscope of Mr. X, see the article "In Memory of Willi Sucher" in *Journal for Star Wisdom 2010.*

11   In Latin, this motto is *Michael-Sophia in nomine Christi;* see Tomberg, *Inner Development,* lecture 1.

such a level as to be almost incomprehensible? It is important to bear in mind, in the context of humankind's spiritual evolution, that evil has the purpose of calling forth the Good. The more one cognizes the extent of evil in the world, the more one is inwardly called to align oneself with the Power of the Good, and this means developing morally and spiritually increasingly *to become*, in one's own being, the Good. In relation to the three great guiding beings—Sophia, Christ, and Michael—there are three aspects to aligning oneself with the Power of the Good. One can align with Sophia, Divine Wisdom, by striving to uphold the fulfillment of the Divine Plan, which is to bring to realization the coming world culture based on Wisdom and Love, known as the Rose of the World. One can increasingly unite oneself inwardly with Christ, Divine Love, as the Bringer of the Power of the Good into the world. And in service of Truth and Justice—this is primarily for those who are called spiritually to become truly active in the struggle against evil—one can align oneself with the Archangel Michael, who is the Upholder of Truth and Justice.

In his lectures on karmic relationships, Rudolf Steiner spoke of a school counter to that of Michael. He referred to it as the school of Ahriman.[12] In the as-yet untranslated chapters of Daniel Andreev's work *Rosa Mira,* or Rose of the World (that is, in the part of this Russian book not yet published in English), the deeper purpose of the existence of the school of Ahriman is revealed. In a wider sense, the school of Ahriman comprises all those souls who have chosen in previous lifetimes, consciously or unconsciously, to ally themselves with Ahriman. As Ahriman is an adversary of Christ, these souls are opposed to Christ, whether they are conscious of this opposition or not. Interestingly, it is possible—at least in some cases—for them to believe they are Christians! Like Hitler, while outwardly proclaiming themselves to be Christians, such individuals nevertheless act and behave in a way that is not aligned with the spirit of Christ or his teachings. As Christ said, "By their fruits you shall know them" (Matthew 7:16)—this is how it is possible to identify whether someone is truly aligned with Christ or is simply using the name of Christ as a convenient label.

12 Steiner, *Karmic Relationships: Esoteric Studies*, vol. 4.

In the school of Ahriman, there are those who can be designated as leaders. These are souls who have advanced far along the path of union with Ahriman and who have thus, in the course of lifetimes, become special protégés of Ahriman. One such soul (that of Stalin) demonstrating a high level of attainment of union with Ahriman is discussed in the unpublished part of *Rosa Mira*. These "leading souls" belonging to the school of Ahriman are those who were/are in the running as candidates for being the human vessel into whom Ahriman will incarnate. According to Daniel Andreev, by the late nineteenth century there were two main candidates in the running. One of them incarnated in 1878 in Georgia and subsequently became leader (*Vozhd*) of the Soviet Union; the other incarnated in Austria in 1889 and became the leader (*Führer*) of Nazi Germany. Commencing around 1933, exactly as predicted by Rudolf Steiner, who, as mentioned, indicated 1933 as the date when the beast would arise, these two individuals, one in the Soviet Union and the other in Nazi Germany, began to engage in a contest as to who could be the most evil—in the sense of being the best instrument of Ahriman—in order to "win the prize" of becoming, in the subsequent incarnation, the vessel for Ahriman's incarnation, Mr. X. While working on the final part of the Russian manuscript *Rosa Mira,* around 1958, Daniel Andreev observed that Stalin had emerged victorious in that contest.

If this is true, the implications are stunning and imply that the hypothesis that the individuality who was incarnated as Stalin and who died on March 5, 1953, reincarnated quickly after a period of less than nine years to be born on February 5, 1962. If this hypothesis is true, then we can expect that this individual will go to great lengths to conceal his identity, as was the case in the life of Joseph Stalin. "Stalin invented much about his life. His official birthday was December 21, 1879...an invented date."[13] The actual date of Stalin's birth was December 6, 1878. His name was also an invention. He did not use the name Stalin—meaning "man of steel"— until 1912. His real name was Josef Vissarionovich Djugashvili. "He was a self-creation. A man who invents his name, birthday,

---

13   Sebag Montefiore, *Young Stalin*, p. 21.

nationality, education and his entire past, in order to change history and play the role of leader..."[14]

Here an important signature—that of deception—is revealed as a key for understanding not only this force in the world but also the modus operandi of that individuality. As Stalin wrote in one of his early articles in *Pravda*, "Fine words are a mask to conceal shady deeds."[15]

In astrosophical research, the date of conception is also considered, which in this case would probably have taken place in May 1961. Jeane Dixon did not give a specific location as the conception or birth place of this human being but indicated that she saw him "born of humble peasant origin" at a location somewhere "in the Middle East," designating the child in her vision as the *Child of the East*. As referred to in the article "In Memory of Willi Sucher" (*Journal for Star Wisdom 2010*), Willi Sucher affirmed, on the basis of his own research, that Jeane Dixon's vision was accurate with regard to the date of birth of the vessel for Ahriman's incarnation, but that he saw the place of birth not in the Middle East but in Africa—more specifically, he referred to Tobruk, Libya, as the place of birth of the human vessel for Ahriman's incarnation.

Returning to the principle of deception as a characteristic associated with this individuality, it is interesting that, in the Islamic tradition, although there is not the specific concept of the Antichrist, there is the concept of the *Dajjal,* or deceiver.[16] "He [the devil]

---

14 Sebag Montefiore, *Stalin: The Court of the Red Tsar*, p. 6.

15 Sebag Montefiore, *Young Stalin*, p. 265. The context of this quote is, "His articles are revealing of his cynical view of diplomacy...and his belief in doublespeak (long before Orwell coined the word): 'A diplomat's words must contradict his deeds...Fine words are a mask to conceal shady deeds.'"

16 Since there is no mention of Christ or Antichrist in the Koran, Muslims originally had no concept of the Antichrist. In the Christian tradition the word Antichrist was first used by John: "Who is a liar but he that denies that Jesus is the Christ? He is the Antichrist" (1 John 2:22). Here, in this use of the word Antichrist by John, the connotation of liar (deceiver) is used and this evidently influenced Muslim understanding. The meaning of the Arabic word *dajjal* was gradually formed. In the course of time, when Muslims heard about the Antichrist of Christian tradition, the word *Dajjal* became identified as this being. In this context the word *dajjal* signifies "deceiver." The root of this word means "to cover something"—for example, "to plate something (a metal) with silver or gold." In former times this word was used

makes promises only to deceive them [the people]" (Qur'an 4:120). Deception is thus a hallmark of this individual. What does deception entail? In the case of Stalin (and the same could be said of Hitler), it is evident that each deceived entire peoples. The primary deception in both cases was the violation of expectations of the general population. This characteristic is very important as a barometer for detecting the personage of the vessel for the incarnation of Ahriman, bearing in mind, as Daniel Andreev pointed out, that the incarnation as Stalin was a preparation for his incarnation as the vessel for Ahriman's incarnation, and that, perfecting his ability to deceive, he would learn from the mistakes he made in his incarnation as the *Vozhd* of the Soviet Union.

The mastery of deception is also referred to by Christ in these words: "False messiahs and false prophets will appear and display great signs and wonders to deceive, if possible, even the elect" (Matthew 24:24). In other words, even Christ's disciples, even members of the school of Michael, are in danger of being deceived by the *Dajjal*, the deceiver. These words highlight the false messiah's mastery of deception. In this connection, these words of Christ are also relevant: "Beware of false prophets, which come to you in sheep's clothing, but inwardly they are ravening wolves" (Matthew 7:15). In these words lies the origin of the term *wolf in sheep's clothing,* which is a perfect description of the *Antilogos*. Both Stalin and Hitler were wolves in sheep's clothing. In fact, the name *Adolf* means "noble wolf," and Hitler was certainly one of the greatest examples ever of a wolf in sheep's clothing, even putting himself forward as a "Christian" in the "sheep's clothing" of Christianity.[17]

---

when a camel owner covered a wounded area of his camel with tar, so that this wound would not be seen by prospective buyers when he took his camel to the bazaar to be sold. This act of covering up was simultaneously an act of deceiving. On this account *dajjal* has the connotation of "deceiving." And since Muslims have learned that the Antichrist of Christian tradition is— among other things—a deceiver, they have associated this already existing word with him and named him *Dajjal*.

17 "The National Socialist State professes its allegiance to positive Christianity. It will be its honest endeavor to protect both the great Christian Confessions in their rights, to secure them from interference with their doctrines, and in their duties to constitute a harmony with the views and the exigencies of

In the case of the coming of the beast of Revelation chapter 13, the term *wolf in sheep's clothing* takes on another level of meaning. The transformation of this human being at the time of Ahriman's incarnation into his human vessel was mentioned earlier. While outwardly appearing to be human, this person will be a vehicle for a higher being (Ahriman), the embodiment of evil on Earth.[18] Here the "sheep's clothing" is the outward appearance of Mr. X as a human being. Behind the outer façade, however, is hidden an evil being intent on leading humankind and the Earth along a path far-removed from the one intended by Christ (Divine Love), Sophia (Divine Wisdom), and Michael (the Guardian of Truth and Justice).

Daniel Andreev (in the part of *Rosa Mira* unpublished in English) depicts in great detail his remarkable visions of the Earth and humanity at the time of the Antilogos/Antichrist (which Rudolf Steiner spoke of as the incarnation of Ahriman). According to Daniel Andreev, it was precisely Stalin's level of union with *Gagtungr*[19] (his possession by Ahriman, or Satan) that is essential to understanding the nature of Stalin's being, something hardly anyone else ever mentions, because in the present age of materialism the concept of *possession* is not taken seriously (see appendix 2). Just to be clear, this is a matter of the highest level of possession by Ahriman. In the case of Hitler, too, who (like Stalin) was far advanced along the path of union with Ahriman and was thus possessed, it is impossible to understand the awesome power he wielded over the hearts and minds of millions of people, unless we also grasp that a higher

---

the State of today"—Adolf Hitler, on June 26, 1934, to Catholic bishops to assure them that he would take action against the new pagan propaganda. "Providence has caused me to be Catholic, and I know therefore how to handle this Church"—Adolf Hitler, reportedly said in Berlin in 1936 on the enmity of the Catholic Church to National Socialism.

18 "Before only a part of the third millennium of the post-Christian era has elapsed, there will be in the West an actual incarnation of Ahriman—Ahriman in the flesh." This prophetic statement relating to the present time was made in a lecture held on November 1, 1919—see Steiner, *The Incarnation of Ahriman*, p. 37.

19 *Gagtungr* in the terminology of Daniel Andreev is the Prince of Darkness known as *Ahriman* in the Persian tradition and as *Satan* in the Judeo-Christian tradition.

being was acting through him. In the case of the possible incarnation on February 5, 1962, of the human vessel (Mr. X) into whom Ahriman incarnates, it is not just a matter of Satan acting through a human being, as took place with Hitler and Stalin; rather it will be for humanity an actual encounter with Ahriman in a person veiled by the mask of his human vessel—veiled to all except to those human beings who are able to see clairvoyantly or behold in clarity of thinking and who will thus not be deceived by this wolf in sheep's clothing. In esoteric terms, whereas Hitler and Stalin were overshadowed by Ahriman (Satan), the "world emperor" will be an actual incarnation of Ahriman in the flesh.

The vista opened up on these mysteries by Daniel Andreev emerges as highly significant in providing us with knowledge concerning the karmic identity of Mr. X and with an understanding of his means of accomplishing his ends. Daniel Andreev refers to three incarnations—that is, earlier lives lived on Earth: one as a Roman emperor (not identified); one as someone active in the Spanish inquisition; and one as Joseph Stalin. Daniel Andreev died at only fifty-two years of age in 1959, thus he did not live to witness the reincarnation of Joseph Stalin on February 5, 1962, the date of that individual's birth in his present incarnation, if the three hypotheses are correct. What he did see, however, was that this individual "will have at his disposal an enormous capacity for work and a multitude of talents.... He will be uniquely and terribly beautiful. From his facial characteristics, it will be difficult to place him in any particular race or nation. Rather, he will be seen as a representative of the collective of humanity."[20]

Further research concerning an earlier incarnation of Stalin is presented by Judith von Halle in her book about life in Palestine at the turning point of time.[21] A whole section in the book is devoted to presenting her research about an earlier incarnation of Stalin as the grandson of Herod the Great. (She says that he was the son of Herod Archelaus, who was a son of Herod the Great.) In her discussion, she also mentions Solovyov's work *A Short Story of the Antichrist.*

---

20 Daniel Andreev, in *Journal for Star Wisdom 2011*, p. 14; see appendix 1.

21 Von Halle, *Vom Leben in der Zeitenwende* (Life at the Turning Point of Time). This book has not yet been published in English.

Apart from this reference, however, there is no other explicit evidence from her in this writing that would indicate whether she is aware of Stalin as the preparatory incarnation to become the vessel for the incarnation of Ahriman. She depicts this grandson of Herod as joining a black (occult) lodge that was, among other things, responsible for the murder of the innocent children in Bethlehem. She indicates that it was from the inspiration that Archelaus's son received in this black lodge that this individuality, when he came to power in his later incarnation as Stalin in the Soviet Union, carried out such heinous deeds. However, she says that this son of Archelaus died at a relatively early age, and that she was unable to find his name, which does not appear to be mentioned in any historical sources. In the Bible, Archelaus is mentioned in the Gospel of Matthew, where it is described how Joseph and Mary fled with the child Jesus to Egypt to avoid the massacre of the innocent children (Matthew 2:13–23). When Herod the Great died, Joseph was told by an angel in a dream to return to Israel, which for Joseph and Mary (who were from Bethlehem) meant returning to Bethlehem.[22] However, upon hearing that Archelaus had succeeded his father as ruler of Judaea, Joseph "was afraid to go thither," and was again notified in a dream to go to Galilee (Matthew 2:22).

If Judith von Halle and Daniel Andreev are correct in their indications of preceding incarnations of Stalin, the following sequence emerges:

1) son of Archelaus—who lived during the first century AD and who died at a relatively early age; (Judith von Halle)

2) Roman emperor—Daniel Andreev does not indicate the name of this emperor or when he lived; however, in order for (1) to hold true as well as (2), it must have been

---

22 In his lecture cycles on the Gospel of Matthew and the Gospel of Luke, Rudolf Steiner describes that there were two families where the parent's names were Joseph and Mary and the child's name was Jesus. The one family, described in the Gospel of Matthew, was from Bethlehem, and the other family, described in the Gospel of Luke, was from Nazareth. See details of the two families, with dates of Jesus' birth and of the key events referred to here, such as the flight to Egypt and the massacre of the innocent children, in Powell, *Chronicle of the Living Christ*.

someone who was Roman emperor later than the first century AD, when the son of Archelaus was living.

3) "The last time that he entered the historical arena [his incarnation preceding that as Stalin] it was in the figure whom Dostoevsky presented with meta-historical acumen as the 'grand inquisitor.' He was no Torquemada. He belonged neither to the highest nor to the lowest ranks of that Satanic experiment [the Spanish inquisition²³]. He appeared as the political wave [of the Spanish inquisition] was already fading away."

The reason for focusing upon that momentous event in this book is to help us prepare for it, to recognize the signature of the ahrimanic forces stepping up their activity on the world stage, and to be in a position to recognize Ahriman behind the mask of the human personage bearing him, so as not to be deceived by this wolf in sheep's clothing. As with Judas, one can feel compassion for Mr. X who, by playing this role, is faced with unimaginable suffering as the karmic consequence of the suffering that during his reign will be inflicted upon humanity and the Earth. In the words of Daniel Andreev: "In the wake of that [incarnation as Mr. X], this individuality will undergo the subsequent catastrophic plunge down into the pit of the galaxy, where all time ceases—into a world of suffering such as, in terms of its hopelessness and relentless intensity, exists nowhere else in the universe."²⁴

How might the inner state of consciousness of Mr. X leading up to the "baptismal event," the great transformation, be described? While our modern materialistic culture has difficulty in conceiving of such an event, other cultures—in their myths and stories handed down by way of tradition—sometimes give indications. One such story from Africa describes an empress invoking a devil goddess, who says to the

---

23   RP: The Spanish inquisition was extremely active during the fifty-year period from 1480 to 1530. For almost one-third of this period, Torquemada, born 1420, was the Grand Inquisitor, from 1483 until his death in 1498. From 1530 to 1560, there were relatively few inquisition trials. Then a further 50,000 trials under the auspices of the Spanish inquisition were registered as having taken place between 1560 and 1700.

24   Quoted from the unpublished part of *Rosa Mira* by Daniel Andreev (that is, the part not yet published in English translation in *The Rose of the World*).

empress: "The price to save your rotten empire is your own miserable self—your life in exchange.... You must give me your body and let me rule your empire, masquerading as you. This means that your soul must leave your body and go to hell, while I enter and act through it. That is my price—take it or leave it."[25] After the devil goddess enters into the empress, "The people of the empire were astonished; never in all their lives had they seen anything like it. Never had they seen a ruler work them so ruthlessly as their new empress."[26] Through this story, we gain some understanding of what transpires at the incarnation of Ahriman and how astonishing will be the consequences of this event for the Earth and humanity. Vladimir Solovyov, in his *Short Story of the Antichrist,* described how, at a certain moment in the life of the human vessel, Satan (Ahriman) bestows his power upon his "only son," who then goes on to rule the world:

> Oh, my beloved son! Let all my benevolence rest on thee!... I have no other son but thee.... Receive thou my spirit! As before my spirit gave birth to thee in beauty, so now it gives birth to thee in power.[27]

If the three hypotheses are correct, it is then possible to draw upon Daniel Andreev's visions of the time of Ahriman's incarnation and, from an understanding of Stalin's personality, to gain some idea of what may be expected when the incarnation of Ahriman takes place. For example, Stalin had at his disposal a vast secret security apparatus, which came to be known as the KGB, a descendant of the secret police known as the *Cheka,* instituted by decree under Lenin.[28] In 1923, the

---

25 Mutwa, *Indaba, My Children: African Folk Tales,* p. 182.

26 Ibid., p. 184.

27 Soloviev, "A Short Story of the Antichrist" (from *War, Progress, and the End of History* (originally published in 1900).

28 After the Bolshevik revolution in October 1917, the first version of the KGB was known as the Cheka (*All-Russian Extraordinary Commission for Combating Counter-Revolution*), a secret police granted the right to undertake quick non-judicial trials and executions, if deemed necessary in order to "protect the revolution." The Cheka became reorganized in 1922 as the GPU (State Political Directorate) and then the OGPU (Joint State Political Directorate) in 1923, while Lenin (1870–1924) was still alive. Under Stalin, in 1934, the OGPU was incorporated into the NKVD (People's Commissariat

Cheka metamorphosed into the OGPU, which conducted Soviet espionage, both nationally and internationally, and later provided Stalin with his chief personal bodyguard. In 1934, the OGPU was incorporated into the NKVD (People's Commissariat of Internal Affairs). The NKVD also took over responsibility for all detention facilities (including the forced labor camps, known as the *Gulag*), as well as for the regular police. Stalin's paranoia led the NKVD to conduct the great purge from 1936 to 1938, involving show trials and political murders of those whom Stalin believed opposed him.

> [Stalin] was old, sclerotic, and forgetful, yet until his death aged seventy-four, on March 5, 1953…remained the peerless politician, paranoid megalomaniac and aberrant master of human misery on a scale only paralleled by Hitlerite Germany. Responsible for the deaths of around 20 to 25 million people, Stalin imagined he was a political, scientific, and literary genius, a people's monarch, a red Tsar.[29]

In our time, the possibilities of surveillance made possible through modern technology exceed anything Stalin could possibly have dreamed of.[30] This fact alone should be a warning to modern human beings never to invest total power in a single individual, who then—as in the case of Stalin—could unleash a reign of terror, utilizing all the far-reaching modern tools of surveillance that have been created since the days of Hitler and Stalin.

It has been foretold (by Rudolf Steiner, Daniel Andreev, and Jeane Dixon) that a time would come, and that time appears to be now, when the forces of *anti-life* (the ahrimanic forces and their human focus, Mr. X) would take hold of the Earth and humanity to such an extent that the very existence of the Earth and humanity would be

---

of Internal Affairs) as the Main Directorate for State Security (GUGB). After various further metamorphoses, this became—after Stalin's death in 1953—the KGB (Committee for State Security) in 1954.

29 Sebag Montefiore, *Young Stalin*, pp. 393–394.

30 Dice, *Big Brother: The Orwellian Nightmare Come True*, details actual high-tech spy gadgets, emerging artificial intelligence systems, and surveillance projects that seem as if they come right out of George Orwell's novel *Nineteen Eighty-Four* (www.markdice.com).

threatened. The ahrimanic forces, working through the human beings belonging to the school of Ahriman, are endeavoring to hijack Mother Earth—and therewith humankind—from the rightful course of evolution guided by Christ and Sophia. The human vessel for Ahriman's incarnation, Mr. X, is the leader of the human beings belonging to the school of Ahriman. Just as Jesus Christ had many disciples, among them the primary twelve disciples, so this individuality will undoubtedly have many devoted followers. Among them, might there be an inner circle of twelve primary disciples who join from the ranks of the rich and powerful? Through their obsessive focus on money and power, concomitant with a total lack of concern for the welfare of the Earth or humanity, Mother Earth is undergoing a crucifixion. What Christ went through on a physical level two thousand years ago can be recognized as enacted now globally on an etheric level. In this apocalyptic battle, we are called to become increasingly wakeful and to make conscious choices on behalf of preserving Life and Love in the world; on behalf of humanity and the Earth, to join forces with the Etheric Christ, aligning ourselves with him and with his bride, Sophia, and with the Archangel Michael and his school, holding in consciousness the future resurrection that will follow this crucifixion.

As this armed combat [of World War I] is one to which nothing in previous history is comparable, so will it be followed by a spiritual struggle to which likewise nothing in history is comparable. (Rudolf Steiner)[1]

What it comes to in the end is this: grasp the power that streams to you in the experience of Christ in the soul and in the powerful regency of his pure spiritual strength. Put on the power of God as one puts on full armor, so that you may stand against the well-aimed attacks of the adversary. For our struggle is not to fight against powers of flesh and blood, but against spirit beings mighty in the stream of time, against spirit beings powerful in the molding of earth substance, against cosmic powers whose darkness rules the present time, against spirits who carry evil into the realms of the spiritual world. Therefore take up the full armor of God, that you may be able to stand your ground on the day when evil unfolds its greatest strength, and victoriously withstand it. Stand firm, then, girded with the truth, like a warrior firmly girded. Connect yourself with all in the world as is justified in the spiritual world, and this connection with the spirit will protect you like a strong breastplate. And may peace stream through you, down to your feet, so that on your path you spread peace, as the message that comes from the realm of the angels. In all your deeds have trust in God. This trust will be like a mighty shield; with it you can quench all the flaming arrows of the evil one. Take into your thinking the certainty of Christ's healing deed. It will protect your head like a helmet. And the spirit, which has become living in you, you shall grasp as one grasps a sharp sword. The sword of the spirit is the working of the Word of God. May this armor clothe you in all your prayers and supplications, so that in the right moment you raise yourself in prayer to the spirit, and at the same time practice wakefulness in inner loyalty. Feel yourself united in prayer with all other bearers of the spirit—also with me, Paul, so that the power of the word will be given to me when I am to courageously bring the knowledge of that holy mystery which lives in the message of the gospel. (Paul's Letter to the Ephesians, 6:10–19)[2]

---

1   Steiner, *Freemasonry and Ritual Work*, p. 449.

2   Based on the translation by John Madsen, *The New Testament: A Rendering*.

CHRIST & THE MAYA CALENDAR
2012—AN UPDATE

In 2009, a book was published that gives some background to what Rudolf Steiner refers to in the quote on page 29 as "a spiritual struggle to which nothing in history is comparable" and for which, of course, we have to be spiritually armed—as expressed in St. Paul's words: "Take up the full armor of God, that you may be able to stand your ground on the day when evil unfolds its greatest strength, and victoriously withstand it." According to the research presented in that book, we are fast approaching "the day when evil unfolds its greatest strength." Since the publication *Christ & the Maya Calendar: 2012 and the Coming of the Antichrist* by Kevin Dann and Robert Powell in 2009, because of the investigative nature of that book, some readers have raised the question as to how the central prognosis outlined in the book can be discerned as an ongoing, encroaching process in the modern world. In response, this book is intended as an update, focusing upon the phenomena visible in the unfolding current events in both the United States and elsewhere that bear the signature of the prophecies explored in the original book, with the proviso that it is not possible to be specific in a very exact way regarding events of this kind, owing to the various imponderables connected with such events.[1]

For those unfamiliar with the book *Christ & the Maya Calendar,* the central theme is about the Second Coming of Christ as the enlivening force of Divine Love in the etheric realm. It also looks at the parallel shadow side of this momentous event, which according to Biblical prophecy is the coming of the Antichrist. It is, in particular,

---

1 See the excellent article "Prophecy: A Cauldron of Controversy" by William Bento in the *Journal for Star Wisdom 2011*, pp. 41–48.

this latter event that we deal with at length in *Christ & the Maya Calendar*, as the subtitle of the book indicates. The following clarification can serve to distinguish between the various names and images associated with the expression *Antichrist*.

The word *Antichrist,* as used in this book and throughout the original book, may be understood in at least two ways. The more general use of the word is found in the Bible and in Christian tradition, in which the Antichrist is understood to be the human being who bears the incarnated Satan (also called *Ahriman* in Persian tradition and in Revelation 13, the *beast*). This is how the word Antichrist is used in the book *Christ & the Maya Calendar*, reflecting the use of the word Antichrist in the prophecies of Biblical tradition and of Jeane Dixon discussed in the book. However, this general meaning should be distinguished from another, more specialized use of the word, as found in the spiritual science of Anthroposophy, which generally uses the word *Antichrist* to designate the Sun Demon known as *Sorath* in the Hebrew tradition, referred to as both the *beast whose number is 666* and as the *two-horned beast* in Revelation 13. In this connection, Rudolf Steiner refers to the two-horned beast as the *false prophet who represents the teachings of the beast.*

The following tabulation is intended to help the reader with respect to these various terms, many of which are synonymous:

THE BIBLE AND CHRISTIAN TRADITION	SPIRITUAL SCIENCE OF ANTHROPOSOPHY
Satan (*Judeo-Christian tradition*)	*Ahriman* (*Persian/Zoroastrian tradition*)
Antichrist = incarnation of Satan	*incarnation of Ahriman*
Antichrist = the beast (Revelation 13)	*the beast (Revelation 13) = incarnation of Ahriman*
the beast whose number is 666 = the two-horned beast	*Sorath, the Sun demon = the Antichrist = the false prophet who represents the teachings of the beast*

Given that the year 2012 is now upon us, it is important to respond to the question just mentioned. The goal of the book *Christ & the Maya Calendar* and of this book, which can be considered an update of that book, is to know the truth in the spirit of the words "You shall know the truth, and the truth shall set you free" (John 8:32), even if the truth is sometimes uncomfortable or inconvenient within the context of our unfolding life and destiny. This book contains an in-depth analysis of what is taking place at the present time through the activity in the world of forces of an anti-Christian nature, offering light-filled perspectives in the section entitled "Future Perspectives" toward the end of this book.

The momentous event of the Second Coming of Christ was prophesied by Rudolf Steiner. In addition, he also prophesied the incarnation of Ahriman into a human being. It is this incarnation of Ahriman into a human being that is called the *coming of the Antichrist* in the Christian tradition. (For Rudolf Steiner, as referred to above, the expression *Antichrist* refers to Sorath, who, among other things, prepares the way for Ahriman's incarnation; see table, page 31.) Essentially, Rudolf Steiner indicated that the Second Coming of Christ is an event taking place in the etheric realm of life forces, and is thus a non-physical manifestation of Christ in an ethereal form, the onset of which he prophesied to start in the year 1933, but which at the same time would entail the beginning of a struggle of apocalyptic dimension with the *beast* in chapter 13 of the Book of Revelation: "Before the Etheric Christ can be comprehended by human beings in the right way, humanity must first cope with encountering the beast who will rise up in 1933."[2]

The authenticity of Rudolf Steiner's prophecy of this twofold event—the return of Christ in an ethereal form and the oppositional event of the arising of the beast that he indicated would begin to be fulfilled in 1933 (some eight years after his death in 1925)—is supported from various perspectives in *Christ & the Maya Calendar*. This theme was further elaborated in the article "World Pentecost" published in the 2010 issue of the *Journal for Star Wisdom* (see appendix 3) and is elucidated from a new perspective later in this book.

In the "World Pentecost" article, the primary focus was upon yet another prophecy made by Rudolf Steiner—one, however, where he did not specify a particular period of time when this might come

---

2   Steiner, *The Book of Revelation and the Work of the Priest*, p. 231.

to fulfillment. In this instance Rudolf Steiner's prophecy is contingent upon a small number of human beings fulfilling a certain condition. The intention in publishing the "World Pentecost" article in the *Journal for Star Wisdom 2010* was to serve toward an awakening of a mood of expectation and "solemn avowal" with respect to the pregnant promise inherent in the unfolding of a World Pentecost.

> If, even in small numbers, human beings make solemn avowal of this, the Pentecost Mystery will take firmer and firmer root in many human beings living at the present time and particularly in the future. Then there will come that which humanity so sorely needs for its redemption and salvation; then the Healing Spirit will speak to a new faculty of understanding in human beings—the Spirit by whom the sickness of human souls is healed, the Spirit sent by Christ. And then will come that which is a need of all humankind: WORLD-PENTECOST![3]

The article "World Pentecost" in the *Journal for Star Wisdom 2010* presented the perspective that the end of the Maya calendar on December 21, 2012 (or on some subsequent date) might possibly be a time when, if human beings would open themselves to the instreaming of Divine Love, Rudolf Steiner's prophecy of World Pentecost might be fulfilled. This perspective is one of a great light-filled event for humanity, as a counter-balance to the dark event prophesied by Rudolf Steiner for our time, which is described in detail in the following. Rudolf Steiner is not the only one to prophecy a coming great light-filled event. At the end of this book, Daniel Andreev's prophecy is mentioned. It indicates that Christ in his Second Coming will appear in heaven surrounded by unspeakable glory: "There will not be a single being on Earth who will not see the Son of God or hear his Word." This glorious event—and also the potential for a World Pentecost—can be borne in mind as the "light at the end of the tunnel" when considering the following. Also it has to be borne in mind that numerous other themes belonging to this update have had to be omitted.

---

3   Steiner, "World Pentecost: The Message of Anthroposophy," lecture of May 17, 1923, in *The Festivals and Their Meaning*.

BOOK OF REVELATION, CHAPTER 13

Central to *Christ & the Maya Calendar* is Rudolf Steiner's indication that scenes depicted in the Book of Revelation are actually mirrored in earthly history. He gave the example that the scene from chapter 12 known as the *war in heaven* was mirrored in earthly history during the period from 1841 to 1879. The exact dating given by Rudolf Steiner of the period from 1841 to 1879 in connection with the war in heaven is an example of translating from the realm of meta-history to that of earthly history. Steiner's indication shows us that the Apocalypse contains a precise account—clothed in magnificent, mythical images—of human history since the first century AD and extending into the distant future, seen from the meta-historical (archetypal) level. Since the war in heaven (1841–1879) is described in the Book of Revelation chapter 12, it follows, logically, that the events in Revelation 13 follow that period chronologically.[4]

One way of reading the images from the Apocalypse is to consider their content as "scenes," rather like in a stage play, unfolding one after the other. Periodically there takes place a change of scene, and a major change of scene generally occurs at the *end* of a chapter in Revelation. The tremendous forces of hindrance that were unleashed into the world through Lenin and Stalin in Russia (and subsequently the whole Soviet Union), through Hitler in Germany (engulfing virtually the whole of Europe), and through Mao in China came to an end, for the main part, with the collapse of Soviet communism in 1991.[5] The end of the communist era in 1991 could be interpreted as one scene—that of the encounter of Sophia with the hindering force of the *red dragon* in communism (the Bolsheviks, for example, called themselves the *reds*, as discussed in *Christ & the Maya Calendar*)—coming to an end, with a new scene in preparation. In this imaginative way of interpreting the sublime visions presented

---

4 Revelation 13 presents a vision of the appearance on the world stage of both the *beast* and the *two-horned beast* whose number is 666 (see table, p. 31).

5 Although China is still officially communist, the world's most populous country began its open-door policy in 1981, and under *laissez faire* capitalism the economy has boomed. This process began just five years after Mao's death in 1976.

in the Book of Revelation, the new scene, signaling a new source of terror on the world stage, opened just ten years later, on September 11, 2001, announcing the transition from chapter 12 to chapter 13 of the Apocalypse.

How may the events of September 11, 2001, be seen to bear the signature of the opening scene to chapter 13 of Revelation on the meta-historical level? Let us go back to the words describing the opening scene of chapter 13: "And I saw a beast rising out of the sea with ten horns and seven heads.... One of its heads seemed to have a mortal wound" (Revelation 13:1-3). Might the "mortal wound" beheld by John a little over nineteen hundred years ago be seen as the "wound" inflicted through the destruction of the twin towers of the World Trade Center, the computer-laden "head" of world trade? In which case, this dramatic event on September 11, 2001, announced to the world the *beast* arising, Satan on his way into incarnation, with one of his heads wounded. Does not the ensuing "war on terror," create the atmosphere needed by the *beast* for his incarnation, keeping humanity in a perpetual state of fear?[6] As mentioned earlier, Revelation 13 is the vision—or series of visions—depicting the incarnation of Satan, referred to in the Apocalypse as the beast. Although Rudolf Steiner used the name *Satan* in early lectures, he subsequently always referred to this being as Ahriman (see the table on page 31.)

Against this background, it could be considered that we are now—since 2001—in an historical period corresponding to Revelation, chapter 13, which creates an atmosphere of fear conducive to the incarnation of Ahriman. Let us consider this event, which is one of the two main themes of this update.[7] Regarding the shadow side of Christ's return, this is referred to in the Christian tradition as the "coming of the Antichrist." Rudolf Steiner, using his own terminology,

---

6   This is not to diminish the significance of the very real threat of terrorism. It is simply to cognize that *fear* is the atmosphere that Satan (also known as Ahriman) feeds on, and thus seeks to create, whereas *love* is the substance that Christ creates and which nurtures and sustains us in our true humanity.

7   The other main theme is that of the return of Christ in the etheric (the Second Coming of Christ)—see my article "2012: Prophecy—Phenomena—Hope," *Journal for Star Wisdom 2012*; see also my article "The Mystery of Christ in Our Time"—http://sophiafoundation.org/articles/

the language of spiritual science, spoke of this as the "incarnation of Ahriman." With this designation, he connected to the Zoroastrian tradition, in which the prince of darkness is referred to as Ahriman. Different cultures use other names for the prince of darkness: for example, the Egyptian tradition spoke of *Seth* (also known as *Typhon*), and the Judeo-Christian tradition speaks of *Satan*. In his apocalyptic work *The Rose of the World*, Daniel Andreev refers to the prince of darkness as *Gagtungr*. Rudolf Steiner distinguished between the spiritual being Ahriman and the human being into whom this spiritual being will incarnate, drawing an analogy with the incarnation of Christ into Jesus. This distinction is not usually made in the Christian tradition, which refers simply to the Antichrist as the human being representing the exact opposite impulse to what came to expression in the incarnation of Jesus Christ.

In the introduction to this book, the individual who serves as the human vessel for the incarnation of Ahriman, or Satan, is designated Mr. X. In the Christian tradition, no distinction is made between the birth of Mr. X and the moment of incarnation of Satan into Mr. X, an event that parallels the incarnation of Christ into Jesus, which took place at the baptism of Jesus in the River Jordan, as described in my book *Chronicle of the Living Christ*. Jeane Dixon, whose prophecy is examined in the book *Christ and the Maya Calendar* and is considered in further detail in this book, refers to the birth of Mr. X to be the *birth of the Antichrist*. Her prophetic vision did not distinguish the *birth of the vessel for the Antichrist*—that is, the *birth of the vessel for the incarnation of Satan* (Ahriman)—from the *baptismal event* of the incarnation of Ahriman (Satan) into his human vessel. Apart from Rudolf Steiner, who is careful to distinguish between the spiritual being Ahriman and the human vessel into whom Ahriman incarnates, none of the general Christian sources—including the Book of Revelation, chapter 13, which refers to this anti-Christian incarnation as the *beast*—make this distinction.

HIJACKING SPIRITUAL EVOLUTION

In the present world a condition of perpetual war, based on fear-mongering owing to the "threat of terror," provides an atmosphere in which a longing arises subconsciously for a "world savior" who will be able to restore peace on Earth. This "world savior," or "world emperor" (known in the Christian tradition as the Antichrist), is discussed in the introduction to this book, where he is referred to as "Mr. X." In the introduction, three prophecies concerning the coming of Mr. X are discussed: that of the Austrian spiritual teacher Rudolf Steiner, who foresaw that the incarnation of Ahriman (Satan) into Mr. X would take place shortly after the year 2000; that of the American clairvoyant Jeane Dixon, who beheld the birth of Mr. X on February 5, 1962 (this date for the birth of Mr. X was confirmed by the great pioneer of astrosophy, Willi Sucher); and that of the Russian poet and seer Daniel Andreev, whose awe-inspiring visions of the coming of the Antichrist (as both he and Jeane Dixon called Mr. X) extend over some two hundred pages of text in the last part of his magnum opus *Rosa Mira*.[8] Daniel Andreev saw in vision the karmic background of Mr. X; his vision showed him that Mr. X would be the reincarnated Stalin, who, together with Adolf Hitler, can be thought of as leading the "school of Ahriman" (to use Rudolf Steiner's expression). Through the astrosophical method of karma research, comparing the horoscope of Mr. X's birth (on February 5, 1962, according to Jeane Dixon and Willi Sucher) with Stalin's horoscope of death (on March 5, 1953), the possibility that Stalin reincarnated on February 5, 1962 to continue his mission in service of Ahriman is shown to be a distinct possibility. The introduction also includes references by Daniel Andreev and Judith von Halle to earlier incarnations preceding that of Stalin.

There is another indication by Daniel Andreev in connection with Stalin that is of great interest, particularly for American readers. In his clairvoyant vision of what took place after Stalin's death, Andreev mentions the soul of Abraham Lincoln—on the side of the

---

8   *Rosa Mira* is the Russian title, translated into English as *The Rose of the World*. The English publication of Daniel Andreev's *Rose of the World*, comprising the first half of *Rosa Mira*, does not contain the Antichrist visions.

forces of the Good—as coming in to help the fallen Stalin. The following is my translation of the relevant passage, in which I have removed expressions used by Daniel Andreev belonging to his unique and special terminology and substituted other, equivalent terms in brackets [ ]:

> In front of the walls of the Russian [subterranean demonic region] there unfolded [against the forces of darkness] one of the greatest battles of the forces of the Russian [saints and beings of Light] united with the Russian [folk spirit], and their forces proved to be insufficient. Angels rushed to help, also [many benevolent supernatural beings] and numerous other illumined transcendental beings. For a while, one of the great illumined human spirits was present there together with the [great company of] instreaming forces at the threshold of [the Russian subterranean demonic region]. On Earth, this great spirit bore the name Abraham Lincoln. Finally, one beheld the galloping horse bearing the White Rider, who, coming from the heights of the World [heavenly region], strove down to the [Russian subterranean demonic region]. Alexander the Blessed [Emperor of Russia from 1801 to 1825], with his weapon, lamed the will of the usurper [Stalin] and then handed him over to the Guardian of Karma. The cries that had filled almost half of [the earthly realm] day and night finally died down. Thereupon, the "plunging one" [Stalin] sank into the magma of the heaviest substance and continued to plunge further down toward the one-dimensional pit of existence.[9]

Against this background, it emerges that there is a spiritual relationship between Stalin and Abraham Lincoln, the latter serving as a source of inspiration—in a good sense, as a benevolent illumined human spirit—for the being of Stalin. In Rudolf Steiner's terminology, Abraham Lincoln, on the side of the forces of the Good, can be viewed as a leading figure belonging to the school of the Archangel Michael, a figure who has taken on the task of assisting the powers of the Good to help save (redeem) the soul of that leader of the school of Ahriman who incarnated as Stalin. Against this background there emerges the activity of the powers of the Good, led by Michael—united with Christ and

---

9   Andrejew, *Rosa Mira*, vol. 3, p. 97 (trans. by RP).

Sophia—in their striving always to assist in the work of redemption of fallen souls, no matter how far a soul may fall.

In tandem with the theme of the incarnation of Ahriman into Mr. X (the reincarnated Stalin, according to Daniel Andreev), there are several related themes—and associated therewith a multitude of phenomena—that deserve to be taken into consideration. The first is Rudolf Steiner's mention of the ahrimanic intention to hijack the Earth and humanity in an endeavor to lead humankind on a path totally different from that of the plan of divine evolution under the guidance of Christ (the Word or Logos) and Sophia (Divine Wisdom), the guiding beings of spiritual evolution, who are referred to in the Book of Revelation as "the Lamb and his Bride." According to Steiner:

> The task of the ahrimanic beings is the following: to prevent the Earth from continuing to develop as it should develop in accordance with the intentions of the divine-spiritual powers with whom humanity is connected from the very outset, inasmuch as humanity is comprised of human souls. (You will find all these things mentioned in my *Outline of Occult Science*). In my *Occult Science* I have spoken of the future development of the Earth, of the Jupiter and Venus phases of evolution: The aim of the ahrimanic powers is to prevent this course of development. Their aim is to harden and freeze up the Earth, to shape it in such a way that, together with the Earth, the human being remains an earthbound creature, becoming hardened, as it were, within earthly substance and continuing to live in the future ages of the world as a kind of statue of the past. These powers thus pursue definite aims, which undoubtedly appear as part of their own individual striving. The Earth could not reach its goal if the ahrimanic powers were to gain victory, if humanity were to become alienated from its beginnings, from the powers who supported humankind at the beginning of its evolution. Outwardly, human beings would develop in a way entirely in keeping with the earthly sphere, but by suppressing their innate disposition which leads them beyond the Earth.[10]

---

10 Steiner, *The Sun Mystery and the Mystery of Death and Resurrection*, lecture of June 11, 1922. Note that the English translation of the passage quoted here is

In accordance with the ideal of the development of a conscious soul activity on the part of modern human beings in order to be able to perceive the forces of good and evil at work in our time, can this elucidation of ahrimanic intention described by Rudolf Steiner be seen in any way as taking effect in today's world? Clearly, one aspect of the ahrimanic intention to hijack evolution involves creating a new race by transforming human beings into ahrimanic beings. What might these ahrimanic human beings be like?

The traditional image of Ahriman is that of the reptilian form of a dragon. He is depicted in numerous icons as being held underfoot by the Archangel Michael. If the reptilian dragon force is imagined not as being underfoot but instead as steadily ascending within, the human being would become inwardly reptilian instead of human. The human being, now having become inwardly ahrimanic, could be imagined as disconnected from higher spiritual cognition, without conscience—cold, calculating, and cunning—with the heart of a sociopath, frozen (ice cold) in the feeling nature, and endowed with a will ruthlessly bent on getting its own way.

In connection with this description of the creation of ahrimanic human beings, it is not only a matter of the ahrimanic intention to reshape humankind according to Ahriman's image and likeness, but also of recreating the whole of nature in order to eliminate from all life the divine spark of creation—this being an *anti-life* impulse. Remarkably, this goal is now possible through technology. By engaging the creative forces of human beings willing to serve toward the creation of an *anti-life* world, the ahrimanic intention appears to be unfolding, whereby the lure for those human beings involved in this undertaking is money and power, with hardly a concern for the well-being of humanity and the Earth. Surely the development of genetically engineered seeds can be recognized as a major ahrimanic "breakthrough" toward the goal of driving out the divine spark from nature? Just as ahrimanically possessed human beings may appear outwardly normal while being cold and reptilian in nature inwardly, so genetically modified crops may appear outwardly to be the same as natural crops,

not taken from this publication but is to be found online—http://wn.rsarchive. org/Lectures/Dates/19220611p01.html - translation revised by RP.

while in reality they are more or less sterile substitutes, lacking the divine spark of existence—the divine spark having been driven out in the forcefully manipulative and invasive process of genetic engineering.

ATMOSPHERIC GEO-ENGINEERING (WEATHER MODIFICATION)

> They will see the Son of Man coming on the clouds of heaven with power and great glory. (Matthew 24:30)

> He was taken up, and a cloud received him out of their sight. And while they looked steadfastly toward heaven as he went up, behold, two angels appeared to them in white apparel, saying, "Men of Galilee, why do you stand gazing up into heaven? This same Jesus, who was taken up from you into heaven, will so come in like manner as you saw him go into heaven." (Acts 1:9–11)

> Behold, he is coming with the clouds; and every eye shall see him. (Revelation 1:7)

These statements from the Bible prophesying Christ's Second Coming all refer to the clouds. What does this signify? According to Rudolf Steiner:

> Through the Mystery of Golgotha, one is able to experience the whole of nature morally. If one gazes up at the clouds and sees lightning flashing down from them, one is able to behold Christ in his etheric form. With the clouds—that is to say, with the elements—he appears in spirit form. This vision may be had by everyone sooner or later.[11]

The large-scale ahrimanic reshaping of the Earth's atmosphere can be seen as a counter-impulse to the event of Christ's Second Coming "in the clouds." This counter-impulse is being carried out by weather modification programs, or atmospheric geo-engineering.[12]

---

11   Steiner, *Freemasonry and Ritual Work*, p. 449.

12   The budget set aside for atmospheric geo-engineering in the United States in the year 2011 alone was 2.7 billion dollars. *Atmospheric geo-engineering* has been defined as "the deliberate large-scale manipulation of the planetary environment to counteract anthropogenic climate change" (The Royal

Largely classified as secret, these programs have been carried out persistently since the 1990s, but are virtually unknown to the general public, since they are rarely reported by the media. In fact, they have been cleverly hidden behind a smokescreen of debunking "hoax propaganda"—the key word used in this debunking propaganda being *chemtrails,* for which the correct term is *persistent contrails*—that classifies all independent research into this field as conspiratorial, thus making it difficult in this realm to separate fact from fiction and beliefs. One researcher who has managed to gather the relevant facts is Rosalind Peterson. Her website CaliforniaSkyWatch.com is an excellent source of scientifically documented factual information concerning the ongoing weather modification programs.[13] There are, moreover, other scientific researchers who, through diligent research, have come to the same or similar conclusions as Rosalind Peterson. As she points out:

> Everyone [has been assured] that persistent jet contrails were normal.... The media (whether television or newspapers) ignored thousands of complaints, allowing our once deep blue skies to be turned into massive jet-produced contrail configurations, white

---

Society 2009). This definition conceals the hidden motivation for atmospheric geo-engineering. According to a report prepared by the Air Force titled "Weather as a Force Multiplier: Owning the Weather by 2025" the U.S. Air Force wants to fully control the weather on Earth by the year 2025— http://theintelhub.com/2011/03/30/secret-presidential-chemtrail-budget-uncovered-exceeds-billions-to-spray-populations-like-roaches/

13 Rosalind Peterson is the California president and cofounder of the Agriculture Defense Coalition (ADC), formed in 2006 to protect agricultural crop production from uncontrolled experimental weather modification programs, atmospheric heating and testing programs, and ocean and atmospheric experimental geo-engineering programs. In 1995, Rosalind became a certified USDA Farm Service Agency Crop Loss Adjustor working in more than ten counties throughout California, finding that many crop losses throughout the State can be attributed to weather related causes. Rosalind earned a BA degree from Sonoma State University in Environmental Studies and Planning (ENSP), with emphasis on agriculture and crop production. As well as Rosalind's website www.californiaskywatch.com, she has another website: www.AgricultureDefenseCoalition.org, which documents scientific evidence of the considerable harm to human health and to the soil and plant life of the Earth caused by the human-made clouds produced by persistent contrails. In September 2007, Rosalind was an invited guest speaker at the United Nations forum on Climate Change.

haze, reflective white particles, various types of man-made clouds, and other unusual formations with varied weather events.... The media deflected questions and real issues into disinformation...against those who raised questions regarding these real events, thereby exacerbating, and allowing to continue, the detrimental effects that man-made clouds are alleged to be having on agriculture, trees, human health, and climate.[14]

A *contrail* (also called a vapor trail) is a visible trail of streaks of condensed water vapor or ice crystals, usually seen forming in the wake of an aircraft passing overhead. Contrails generally dissolve fairly rapidly, within a matter of minutes. A persistent contrail, which forms because of aerosol spraying from the plane, is abnormal. The persistence of the contrail is a sign that it contains chemicals or other elements that prevent the contrail from dissolving as it would do normally. These persistent contrails lead to the formation of human-made clouds laced with chemicals or other elements. The increasing cloud coverage of the Earth's atmosphere, according to a March 2, 2006, BBC news report, leads to the conclusion that "ground-based astronomy could be impossible within forty years."[15] This is of serious concern for everyone interested in viewing the stars, not to mention the devastating impact upon all human, animal, and plant life by the more-or-less permanent disappearance of the Sun behind a covering of cloud.

Atmospheric geo-engineering bears the signature of an ahrimanic intervention, an active opposition to the Second Coming of Christ—his "coming in the clouds" (Revelation 1:7). Whereas Christ is now active in the Earth's etheric aura ("in the clouds") as a life-bestowing *Presence* (Greek: *Parousia*) for humanity and the Earth, this ahrimanic intervention entails a long-term program to radically change the Earth's atmosphere through aerosol spraying from jet planes, creating persistent contrails that form human-made clouds. The title

---

14 Rosalind Petersen, "Persistent Jet Contrails & Man-Made Clouds Change Our Climate, Harming Agriculture & Our Natural Resources"—http://newswithviews.com/Peterson/rosalind117.htm Throughout this book, comments inserted by the author in quotations are denoted by brackets [ ].

15 http://news.bbc.co.uk/2/hi/science/nature/4755996.stm

of Rosalind Peterson's article quoted here ("Persistent Jet Contrails and Man-Made Clouds Change Our Climate, Harming Agriculture and Our Natural Resources") expresses the ahrimanic goal to harm humanity and the Earth, which is the exact opposite of the work of the Etheric Christ in the Earth's ethereal aura for the benefit of Mother Nature and humankind.

Rudolf Steiner spoke some ninety years ago about this intervention in the world of nature as a plan to take control of natural processes and the beings active in these processes, the nature spirits or elemental beings:

> This entire choir of beings [gnomes, undines, sylphs, salamanders] is just as much around us as are stones, plants, animals, and physical human beings. This whole choir can either approach us, revealing itself, in that we now willingly take up the spiritual, or it can shut itself out of our consciousness. If we do not want to know anything about the spiritual world, then this entire choir comes under the sway of ahrimanic powers. Then a covenant between Ahriman and the nature spirits takes place. At the present time, this is what looms as an overriding decision [on the part of the ahrimanic powers], to bring about a union between the ahrimanic powers and the nature spirits. There is a kind of compromise underway between the ahrimanic powers and the nature spirits. And there is no other possibility of hindering it than this: human beings must turn to the spiritual world for spiritual knowledge and thereby get to know the nature spirits, just as we know about oxygen, nitrogen, hydrogen, calcium, sodium, and so on. Alongside the scientific exploration of the sense-perceptible, physical levels, there has to be a science of the spiritual, which has to be taken absolutely seriously.[16]

Against this background, it is clear that a response to the ahrimanic intervention into the processes of nature is twofold: initially to realize that a battle for control of nature is taking place, then to ally

---

16 Steiner, *The Sun Mystery and the Mystery of Death and Resurrection*, lecture of June 11, 1922 (The translation here is by RP and differs from the published book).

oneself with the Etheric Christ, who offers a different way of working together with the elemental beings:

> Without warning, a furious storm came up on the lake, so that the waves swept over the boat. But Jesus was sleeping. The disciples went and woke him, saying, "Lord, save us! We're going to drown!" He replied, "You of little faith, why are you so afraid?" Then he got up and rebuked the winds and the waves, and it was completely calm. The men were amazed and asked, "What kind of man is this? Even the winds and the waves obey him!" (Matthew 8:24–27)

Here the power of Divine Love (Christ) is revealed. It has the power to calm the winds and the waves. In other words, the elemental beings respond to the voice of Divine Love. This is what the Etheric Christ is seeking to teach human beings at the present time, at least, to those who are receptive. Here there is a completely free and loving relationship with the elemental beings, whereas the opposite is revealed by the poisoning of the Earth's atmosphere and soil and by the genetic manipulation of seeds. Atmospheric geo-engineering and the genetic manipulation of seeds are activities that bear the stamp of an ahrimanic intervention into the etheric realm of life forces in order to exercise total control over nature and all the elemental beings, just as Steiner had warned of when he spoke in 1922 of the possibility of the entire choir of elemental beings coming under the sway of ahrimanic powers. In relation to this endeavor human beings are called to participate in the daily activity of choosing life over anti-life. It is a matter of deciding to ally oneself with the Etheric Christ, to participate in his work of Love in the creation of a New Earth where, eventually, the elemental beings will be liberated.[17]

Rudolf Steiner expresses this work of Love, united with Christ, in these words:

> When one discovers oneself within one's innermost sanctuary, one will be allowed to enter in and there discover the Holy

---

17 See *Meditations on the Tarot* (trans. RP), chapter 3, where this theme is addressed, particularly regarding the moral and spiritual prerequisites for participating in this sacred work of Christ known as *sacred magic*.

Grail.... One enters the Mystery Center of one's own heart and a divine being emerges from this place and unites itself with the God outside, with the Being of Christ.... Because the human being is a twofold being, one is able to pour the Sun forces into the Earth and act as a connecting link between the Sun and the Earth.... It is the mission of every single human being and the whole of humanity to fill themselves with the Christ Spirit and to recognize themselves as a center living in this Spirit, through which spiritual light, spiritual strength, and spiritual warmth can flow into the Earth, thereby redeeming it and raising it aloft into spiritual realms.[18]

To consciously align oneself with Christ as a deed of free will or to fall unconsciously under the sway of ahrimanic forces—this is the choice facing humanity now. The essence of this decision is expressed in a meditation on the Etheric Christ communicated by the Russian esotericist Valentin Tomberg (1900–1973) at Easter 1941: "Christ is already here; from the south of the Earth, waves are proceeding from him across the world. Every human being is now able to create a connection with him. The human being has to do this out of free will."[19] This meditation goes on to refer to two streams active in the etheric realm: the radiant blue stream of the Etheric Christ and the opposing ahrimanic stream of the Antichrist.[20] One aspect of aligning oneself with Christ in the great battle with the forces of his adversary entails awakening to cognition of the hardening forces of anti-life now manifesting in the world. The purpose of this book is to assist in the awakening of this consciousness, which is a significant first step in the battle—a necessary step according to Rudolf Steiner, in order for Christ to prevail. First *diagnosis*, then *activation of the will* to find a suitable healing course of action as a response to the situation.

---

18 Steiner, *Freemasonry and Ritual Work*, p. 430. (The translation here is by RP and differs slightly from the published version).

19 In Powell & Dann, *Christ & the Maya Calendar*, p. 217.

20 Ibid. In this meditation concerning the Etheric Christ and the opposition to him stemming from his adversary, the Antichrist, the wording of the meditation leaves it open to interpretation in which sense the Antichrist is referred to (see the table on page 31 for the two interpretations).

Against the background of this battle, there is still another dimension to the weather modification programs (atmospheric geo-engineering) to be considered. In Revelation 13, we read: "[The two-horned beast] performed great and miraculous signs, even causing fire to come down from heaven to Earth in full view of men."[21] Could it be that these prophetic words from Revelation are coming to realization in our time, now that there is the possibility of creating artificial bolts of lightning through laser technology to come down from the atmosphere "in full view of men"? While the Book of Revelation does not go into the consequences of technologically generated lightning coming down, it is possible that artificially created high energy "lightning" in the form of laser beams could precipitate all kinds of catastrophes such as hurricanes, earthquakes, cyclones, massive rain storms with subsequent flooding, and so on, whereby the "lightning" causing these weather phenomena could either remain invisible or could manifest itself under certain conditions. Such technology generating artificial "lightning" could be directed against very specific targets at far-distant locations around the Earth, causing "natural catastrophes." Could it be that such catastrophic events brought about in this way fulfill the prophecy of the "dark miracles" spoken of by Daniel Andreev that he said would shatter "the consciousness of human beings to the very roots of their being?"[22] Through the implementation of such a "lightning-making machine," devastating catastrophes could be induced, appearing as though they were natural disasters.

The military's effort to gain total control over the world's weather,[23] the weaponized application of a "lightning generating" machine used in conjunction with the plasma-like condition of the Earth's atmosphere created by atmospheric geo-engineering

---

21 Revelation 13:13: "Fire to come down from heaven" can be understood phenomenologically as *lightning*, or something akin to lightning—such as a laser beam, for example.

22 Quoted from Andreev, "The Rose of the World," in *Journal for Star Wisdom 2011*, p. 14; see appendix 1.

23 According to a report prepared by the Air Force titled "Weather as a Force Multiplier: Owning the Weather by 2025" the U.S. Air Force wants to fully control the weather on Earth by the year 2025—http://the intelhub. com/2011/03/30/secret-presidential-chemtrail-budget-uncovered-exceeds-billions-to-spray-populations-like-roaches/

could have catastrophic consequences for the entire Earth and all humankind. Certainly, global weather patterns are changing rapidly. Could it be that through the ongoing weather modification programs, the Earth's atmosphere—and hence also global weather patterns—is now changing rapidly, becoming influenced to become *conductive*, creating plasma channels for the global weaponization of the Earth's atmosphere as a conducting vessel for military purposes? Could it be that a super lightning-making machine as alluded to in chapter 13 of the Book of Revelation causing "fire to come down from heaven" is already in use by the military?

This prophecy from the Book of Revelation has to be taken seriously, and all the signs are that it has already been fulfilled. Without going into further details here, owing to lack of space, recent research indicates that behind the scenes a vast battle is taking place involving the entire Earth, which, because of the Second Coming, the appearance of Christ in the etheric realm, could now be developing into a *Grail Temple* for the Etheric Christ. The Earth is under siege because of the opposing forces described in this book, including—as a potential "mastermind" of the endeavor on the part of the military to gain total control over the world's weather by the year 2025—the possibility of a strategically placed machine representing an *Anti-Grail* technology, capable of causing death and destruction without people even knowing of its existence.

Since the 1970s, researchers have attempted to trigger lightning strikes by means of directing pulses from extremely powerful lasers sending several terawatts into the clouds to call down electrical discharges.[24] The laser beams make *plasma channels* of ionized molecules ("filaments"). The filaments lead electricity through the clouds, playing the role of lightning rods. Against this background we see why there is a hidden military agenda to generate human-made clouds all around the Earth. A mega lightning-making machine at a strategic location directing high energy laser beams up to the ionosphere and

---

24 See http://en.wikipedia.org/wiki/Lightning. A terawatt is one trillion watts; a gigawatt is one billion watts; a megawatt is one million watts. See also "Lasers Trigger Lightning Precursors in Clouds" in the *National Geographic News* issue for April 16, 2008—http://news.nationalgeographic.com/news/2008/04/080416-lightning-lasers.html.

bouncing the beams back down from the ionosphere to specific locations on the Earth could utilize the plasma-like conditions created by the human-made clouds for triggering extreme weather conditions upon the Earth (earthquakes, torrential rain, and so on), even making use of other grid systems—although the frequencies would have to be modified to accomplish this, which is, nevertheless, not beyond the bounds of possibility.[25]

GLOBAL ELECTROMAGNETIC GRID

In addition to the global atmospheric grid currently being created through weather modification programs, and in addition to the World Wide Web (WWW) of computers linked via the Internet, there is now also the striving toward a World Wide Electromagnetic Grid of mobile (cell) phones and cell phone towers. Such a grid offers the possibility for new levels of surveillance and other undreamt-of possibilities of ahrimanic intervention into human life. The following, from a scientific paper about the World Wide Electromagnetic Grid and its potentials, indicates the possibility of encouraging "reporting on people" as

---

25   One of the signs that the prophecy of Revelation 13 about causing "fire to come down from heaven" has already been fulfilled in the form of some kind of ahrimanic lightning-making machine placed at a strategic location and bringing about devastating catastrophes, making them appear as natural disasters, is the stunning increase in the number of earthquakes happening around the world. The United States Geological Survey (USGS) website indicates that there were 16,612 earthquakes worldwide in 1990. In the 1990s the number of earthquakes began to rise rapidly, so that by 2003 the number had almost doubled. The USGS website indicates that there were 31,366 earthquakes worldwide in 2003. Increased solar activity is often put forward as an explanation for the dramatic increase, but the number of solar flares occurring annually does not directly correlate with the yearly incidence of earthquakes. There is clearly some other factor at work, which might point to the implementation of a lightning-making machine causing earthquakes (among other "natural catastrophes"), an implementation that evidently began during the 1990s—particularly since the USGS website shows a fairly steady rate of earthquakes in the period prior to 1990 and in the early 1990s. The really dramatic increase in the number of earthquakes began in 2001, exactly the year in which (on September 11, 2001) the transition from Revelation 12 to 13 began, according to the Apocalypse code discussed in chapter 2 of *Christ & the Maya Calendar*.

was widely practiced in Nazi Germany and in the Soviet Union—now using cell phones or other personal digital assistants:

> Nowadays, cell phones and personal digital assistants are equipped with many facilities such as digital camera, audio recorder, mp3 player, video recorder and GPS. In addition, the connection of such devices has improved in the recent past and now it is possible to use messaging services such as EMS and MMS, and access the WWW. We can imagine examples of VOs [Virtual Organizations] such as for Terrorist Detection. In this scenario, a citizen who has seen some suspicious person or fact in an area of public access, such as a tram, train station or a shopping mall, could initiate a short-term VO for analyzing and checking the potential attack. The formation process of the VO begins when the user contacts a counter-terrorist service. This service will be responsible for taking over the evolution of the VO and leading the necessary participants. The necessary people should be included by the counter-terrorism service for evaluating and checking the facts.[26]

In addition to the move toward establishing a World Wide Electromagnetic Grid, there is also an endeavor to set up a Smart Meter Grid, whereby each home is equipped with a smart meter fitted with two antennae for controlling and monitoring the electricity used in each household. "The smart electric grid may be just a little too smart. Once a smart meter is attached to a home, it can gather a lot more data than just how much electricity a family uses. It can tell how many people live in the house, when they get up, when they go to sleep, and when they aren't home."[27] One antenna is used to transmit information back to the power company[28] and the other antenna (by and large, not

---

26 Marcos Dias de Assunção and Rajkumar Buyya, "A Case for the World Wide Grid: Interlinking Islands of Grids to Create an Evolvable Global Cyberinfrastructure"; *www.cloudbus.org/reports/wwg_case.pdf*.

27 Koehle, *Just Say No To Big Brother's Smart Meters: The Battle Against Smart Meters, Their Harmful, Untested RF Emissions and Other Forms of EMF—Electromagnetic Frequency Emissions*; www.nosmartmeters.net offers a free download of this highly informative book.

28 This one antenna alone is incredibly powerful. It emits high, sharply spiked pulses of microwave radio frequency radiation every one to two minutes.

yet activated) is set up to transmit microwave radio frequency radiation into households. The exposure to electromagnetic radiation being pulsed into one's home is inimical to the human etheric (life) body, and thus hooking up in this way to the global electromagnetic grid signifies exposing oneself to an influence that not only saps one's life energy but is positively harmful—"We are dealing with microwave radiation that is an environmental toxin."[29] Moreover, some of the detrimental effects listed in the footnote below seem to indicate that the influence of smart meters goes beyond the etheric level to the soul level—and perhaps their influence extends even beyond this to a spiritual level.

In face of all that is now transpiring, how are we as human beings to compensate for the diminishing life energy, loss of memory, and so on that we owe to increasing exposure to electromagnetic radiation and other forms of radiation? And how are we ever to make good for the devastating impact upon the Earth's etheric body through subjecting it to the incredibly high levels of electromagnetic radiation coming from satellites, cell phone towers, and so on—an impact that

---

Measurements indicate that the radiation is up to one thousand times stronger than that of a cell phone. This is equivalent to seventeen hours of cell phone usage a day for each meter. This amount is increased enormously in the case of businesses, office buildings, and apartment complexes, which have large clusters of meters mounted together. No wonder that since the installation of smart meters in more than seven million homes in California, thousands of people have become ill with one or more of these symptoms: aches and pains, burning sensations in the head or different parts of the body, dry lips, buzzing sounds in the ears, headaches, nausea, insomnia, rapid heart palpitations, waking up in the middle of the night at precisely the same time for weeks on end, emotional instability, inner sense of agitation, skin rashes, difficulty in speaking, loss of memory, inflammation of the ears, a sense of electrification of the brain, sensations of receiving electric shocks in the head and different parts of the body, high pitched sounds in the ears, fatigue, exhaustion, dizziness, heavy crushing pressure on the chest, palpitations, arrhythmias, feeling weak at the knees, cardiac symptoms, migraines, chest tightness, difficulty in opening the eyes in the morning, pressure in the ears, stabbing pains in the neck and shoulders, neuropathy (nerve damage), ringing in the ears, etc., to name a number of the symptoms that people are experiencing as a consequence of the installation of smart meters at their homes.

29 Sandi Maurer of the EMF Safety Network—www.emfsafetynetwork.org. For an excellent overview, see also the article "The Problems with Smart Grids: Dumb & Dangerous" by Blake Levitt and Chellis Glendinning - http://www.culturechange.org/cms/content/view/714/63/

has (among other things) led to the destruction of a high percentage of the bee population?[30]

On the other hand, let us always hold in consciousness that Christ is now active in the Earth's etheric aura, awakening humankind's sense of morality with respect to nature:

> Now, through the Mystery of Golgotha, one is able to experience the whole of nature morally. If one gazes up at the clouds and sees lightning flashing down from them, one is able to behold Christ in his etheric form. With the clouds—that is to say, with the elements—he appears in spirit form. This vision may be had by everyone sooner or later.[31]

On the one hand, humanity can now choose—in freedom—to align with the activity of the Etheric Christ, thereby experiencing "the whole of nature morally." On the other hand, given that humanity is now also in a period of preparation for the incarnation of Ahriman, it is clear that the use of a lightning-making machine in service of the beast could be expected in our time as a fulfillment of the vision of the future revealed in Revelation 13. At the same time it is clear that any ahrimanic "lightning" generated by way of using advanced laser technology is in direct opposition to Christ's Second Coming, which is alluded to in these words: "For as *lightning* comes out of the east, and shines even unto the west, so shall also the coming of the Son of Man be" (Matthew 24:27).

Ultimately, it is Christ who is the source of the apocalyptic visions revealed in the last book of the Bible, and as Christ said of himself: "I am the way, the *truth*, and the life," the visions belonging to the Book of Revelation can be trusted. Nevertheless, they need to be correctly understood and interpreted. In this respect the *Apocalypse code* is a helpful guide.[32]

---

30 Warnke, *Bees, Birds and Mankind: Destroying Nature by 'Electrosmog'— Effects of Wireless Communications Technologies.*

31 Steiner, *From the History & Contents of the First Section of the Esoteric School 1904–1914*, p. 281.

32 Powell, "The Apocalypse Code," *Christian Star Calendar 2009*, pp. 11–18. See also chapter 2 of *Christ & the Maya Calendar.*

From the Apocalypse code it emerges that there is truly an apocalyptic battle taking place at the present time—a battle between the Etheric Christ and his hosts on the one hand and Ahriman and the ahrimanic powers on the other. This battle is being fought on many levels. While the Etheric Christ is streaming into the Earth's etheric aura in radiant light extending down to the heart of the Earth (Shambhala), which is the center of the Earth's etheric body, there is a counter impulse: the ahrimanic plan to create a global grid utilizing the subearthly forces of electricity, electromagnetism, and radioactivity, as well as exerting a direct influence upon human thinking by way of streaming out "thought influences" seeded into human minds, for which the global computer network is the primary vehicle.[33] The essence of this battle in terms of its effect on human beings could be summarized as "radiation coming from without"—whether it be radioactive, electromagnetic, electrical, or mental (mind control)—versus the "radiation from within" arising through Christ's light, love, life, and peace radiating from within the human being. The inner radiance (radiation) of Christ is protection against the outer radiation from the ahrimanic powers. And here, in relation to this battle, human beings can choose which side to be on.[34] It is possible to unite with the global influence of the

---

33 There are numerous examples via the Internet and also, of course, through sophisticated advertising methods, which make use of "thought influences." These methods can be relatively easily adapted for the purpose of directly influencing the human mind, if human beings are unsuspecting and not prepared to resist such influences. There is considerable evidence that mind control is now practiced on a widespread scale—see Dice, *Big Brother: The Orwellian Nightmare Come True*; www.MarkDice.com. The use of mind control by the Antichrist is referred to by Daniel Andreev in these words: "Under the Antichrist...psychic control will already stifle such thoughts [of opposition] as soon as they arise, and only a few will succeed in acquiring a system of psychic self-defense which will protect them from being physically destroyed" (Andreev, "The Rose of the World," in *Journal for Star Wisdom 2011*). In the next footnote some indications are given regarding practices that can help protect against the influence of mind control.

34 Powell, *The Morning Meditation in Eurythmy: Four Levels of Bringing to Realization "Not I but Christ in Me"* gives instruction in the schooling of the stream of inner radiance through connecting with the Etheric Christ through the etheric form of movement known as *eurythmy*, which is also the endeavor of all the workshops and activities of the Choreocosmos School of Cosmic and Sacred Dance under the auspices of the Sophia Foundation of North America—www.sophiafoundation.org. Choreocosmos, which is one

Etheric Christ and become part of his endeavor on behalf of the Earth and humanity—or, if the step of uniting with the Etheric Christ is not taken consciously, similar to the fate of the elemental beings as described above by Rudolf Steiner, by default the Ahriman powers will then hold sway over human beings, the elemental beings, and the life processes of the Earth. The words "Not I, but Christ in me" are a significant key in linking up to Christ's light-filled realm as opposed to unwittingly falling prey to the influence of the grid (or grids) central to the ahrimanic plan. For example, the Smart Meter Grid—at least in the United States—appears to be moving ahead, perhaps intended to be in place by the time of Ahriman's incarnation into his human vessel, Mr. X.[35]

MACHINE ASSAULT ON NATURE

What is our protection in the great struggle with the forces of evil? And what might be the primary sources of inspiration in linking with the Etheric Christ within the context of the great apocalyptic struggle of our time? These two questions are of key significance. As stated by Judith von Halle in the quotation from one of her books cited in the introduction to this book:

> [The] first task is to devote [oneself] entirely to the Christ Mystery with all [one's] thinking, feeling, and will. This Christ Mystery, however, inevitably encompasses the Mystery of His adversary. The esoteric pupil could not learn to grasp the deeds of Christ—both those at the turning point of time and those of the contemporary Christ being today—and could never develop a fuller understanding of the Christ being and His significance for future human evolution, let alone find the path

---

of the ways offered as a path in our time toward uniting with the Etheric Christ, also affirms the cosmic nature of the human being—the relationship of the human being to the whole cosmos—which is threatened at this time by the intervention of the ahrimanic powers.

35 A great many people in California are actively resisting the installation of smart meters on their homes, one of the ways being through installing an anti-vandalism cage around their existing meter—see Koehle, *Just Say No To Big Brother's Smart Meters*.

to redemption...[without] also enquir[ing] into all that seeks to prevent [one] from following [the] Redeemer.[36]

These words can be a source of inspiration in linking with Christ within the context of the great apocalyptic struggle of our time, and toward the end of this book, in the section entitled "Future Perspectives," further indications are given.

So far in this book, phenomena associated with three significant contemporary themes, which are symptomatic of this apocalyptic struggle—the genetic manipulation of seeds, weather modification (atmospheric geo-engineering), and the global grid in its various forms—have been considered. We now come to a fourth related theme, which is referred to by Daniel Andreev with these words: "When the machine civilization begins its total assault on nature, the entire landscape of the Earth's surface will be transformed into a complete anti-nature."[37] The three preceding themes, each in their own way, also portray aspects of the "total assault on nature"—in the first instance through genetically modified crops which, in the space of a few years, by leeching the soil of its vital nutrients, are capable of transforming fertile agricultural land into something akin to a lunar landscape.[38] The far-reaching devastation of nature now underway through the weather modification programs has already been discussed. In addition, Rosalind Peterson

---

36 Von Halle, *Descent into the Depths of the Earth*, pp. 49–50. Concerning Judith von Halle, see *Christ & the Maya Calendar*, appendix 2.

37 Quoted from Andreev, "The Rose of the World," in *Journal for Star Wisdom 2011*, p. 14; see appendix 1.

38 Engdahl, *Seeds of Destruction: The Hidden Agenda of Genetic Manipulation*, p. 186: For more than a century, Argentine farm land, especially the legendary pampas, had been filled with wide fields of corn and wheat amid green pastures grazed by herds of cattle. Farmers rotated between crops and cattle to preserve soil quality. With the introduction of soybean monoculture, the soil, leeched of its vital nutrients, required even more chemical fertilizers— not less, as Monsanto had promised. The large beef and dairy herds which had roamed freely for decades on the grasslands of Argentina were now forced into cramped U.S.-style mass cattle feedlots to make way for the more lucrative soybean. Fields of traditional cereals, lentils, peas, and green beans have already almost vanished. A leading Argentine agro-ecologist, Walter Pengue, a specialist in the impact of GMO soybeans, predicted that, "If we continue in this path, perhaps within fifty years the land will not produce anything at all."

has also drawn attention to the military programs now underway off the Pacific and Atlantic coasts of the United States to "harass, harm, pursue, hunt, shoot, wound, kill, trap, capture, or collect" millions of marine animals, as well as the dumping of highly toxic chemicals by the military into the waters of the Pacific and the Atlantic, which will contaminate not only the water but also the air and soil.[39] And the effect of electromagnetic radiation on nature—for example, the devastating impact on bees—has also been mentioned (see footnote 32). Over and above these three anti-life themes, there are some other very direct examples of what Daniel Andreev calls the "machine civilization's total assault on nature."

One such striking recent example of the assault of machine civilization on nature is the British Petroleum oil spill that took place in the Gulf of Mexico in 2010. During a three-month period, after the explosion of the Deepwater Horizon offshore drilling unit on April 20, 2010, some five million barrels of oil gushed out into the Gulf of Mexico causing far-reaching devastation:

> The total amount of Louisiana shoreline impacted by oil grew from 287 miles in July to 320 miles in late November 2010. In January 2011, an oil spill commissioner reported that tar balls continue to wash up, oil sheen trails are seen in the wake of fishing boats, wetlands marsh grass remains fouled and dying, and that crude oil lies offshore in deep water and in fine silts and sands onshore. A research team found oil on the bottom of the sea floor in late February 2011 that did not seem to be degrading. Skimmer ships, floating containment booms, anchored barriers, sand-filled barricades along shorelines, and dispersants were used in an attempt to protect hundreds of miles of beaches, wetlands, and estuaries from the spreading oil. Scientists have also reported immense underwater plumes of dissolved oil not visible at the surface as well as an eighty-square-mile "kill zone" surrounding the blown well.[40]

---

39 See www.AgricultureDefenseCoalition.org, Rosalind Peterson's website that documents military plans for the Atlantic and Pacific coasts of the U.S.

40 See http://en.wikipedia.org/wiki/: Deepwater_Horizon_oil_spill

In addition to the assault on nature, wide-ranging health effects—for example, through exposure to hydrogen sulfide—accompanied and continue to accompany the oil spill disaster, which has been spoken of as the largest human-caused catastrophe of all time. There is much more that could be said in connection with the BP oil spill in the Gulf of Mexico—for example, the willful negligence that led to the explosion—which justifies including this disaster in the category of the "machine civilization's total assault on nature." The year 2010 thus seems to belong to the period of time prophesied by Daniel Andreev as the time when this total assault would be underway—as does the year 2011 with the catastrophe in Japan at the Fukushima nuclear power plant in the wake of the 9.0 magnitude earthquake that struck forty-five miles east of Japan's Oshika Peninsula on the afternoon (at 2:46 pm local time, equating with 5:46 am Universal Time) of March 11, 2011, which triggered an extremely destructive *tsunami* with waves up to seventy feet high. Within minutes the *tsunami* struck Japan causing wide-ranging destruction and leading to some 25,000 deaths (dead or missing). In terms of the incredible amount of damage caused by the tsunami, it is claimed to be the most expensive natural catastrophe of all time. And the highly dangerous leaking of radioactivity from the Fukushima nuclear plant has prompted a worldwide reassessment concerning the danger of the nuclear option for meeting humanity's energy needs.[41] Many further incidents could be cited regarding the "total assault on nature" prophesied by Daniel Andreev for this time. And many other themes could be addressed, showing ahrimanic anti-life forces at work on the Earth at the present time.

AHRIMANIC MAYA

Another important theme is that of the creation of an ahrimanic *maya,* into which a large part of humankind is being drawn. The Sanskrit word *maya* is an age-old concept that describes what is now

---

41 At the time of writing, the extent of damage through radioactivity from the Japanese nuclear plants, and the possibility of an extremely large number of deaths in relation to the "Japan situation" cannot be properly assessed. This truly apocalyptic scenario is likely to be far more devastating than the Gulf Oil spill of 2010.

taking place in our world (*deception* also being a key word here). For the *rishis* of Ancient India, *maya* signified the illusion we come into by virtue of forgetting our spiritual origin and, in forgetting, that we come to believe in sense perceptible reality as a given, replacing spiritual reality. In the ancient Greek period, we find a culmination of this dichotomy with Plato and Aristotle. Plato points back ("up") to spiritual reality as primary; Aristotle points the way forward ("down") to learning from sense-perceptible reality.[42] Now, in our own era, Rudolf Steiner and others, through spiritual science, point the way back (actually *forward*) from sense-perceptible reality to spiritual reality. At the same time, though, a counter-impulse is manifesting with ever greater strength: this is an ahrimanic *maya* created by those in power, aided and abetted by the media armed with a whole battery of possibilities offered by modern technology to create a *virtual reality*. The same admonition applies now as it did in Ancient India: *discernment* is the first step on the spiritual path. If discernment is not applied to see through the veil of the new ahrimanic *maya*, a large part of humanity (those who are deceived by this *maya*) will be ensnared in a descending path, leading ultimately into Ahriman's realm (known to ancient Greeks as *Hades* and to ancient Israelites as *Sheol*). One does not have to be clairvoyant to see that in its beginning stages this is actually happening now. Fortunately, through the guiding forces of spiritual evolution there is a beacon of spiritual light and truth to help us discern. We must focus on the light of spiritual truth and, where possible (in response to questions, for example, or where there is a heart opening), allow the light of spiritual truth to shine into the lives of others, particularly now, when so many are being taken in by the ahrimanic *maya*.

Going even beyond *virtual reality*, there are new technologies assisting in the creation of ahrimanic *maya* currently being developed at a breathtaking pace. In fact, for some, *virtual reality* is now quite *passé*, having been completely eclipsed by *augmented reality* (AR), which is defined this way: "*Augmented reality* combines real and

---

42 Plato (pointing up) and Aristotle (pointing forward and down) are represented by the Italian Renaissance painter Raphael in his great work *The School of Athens* in the Vatican museum in Rome.

virtual, is interactive in real time, and is registered in 3-D."[43] Clearly, Ahriman's plans for ensnaring humankind in what is described in *Christ & the Maya Calendar* as the *third temptation* (that of *turning stones into bread*—for example, through virtual and augmented reality) are proceeding with great rapidity.

With the help of the media and modern technology, human beings are being drawn into an ahrimanic *maya*. This is a very serious problem, having an enormous impact upon humanity's spiritual evolution at the present time. It is preparing the way for the greatest deception ever perpetrated upon a (largely unsuspecting) public—at least, upon those who believe in the veil presented by the ahrimanic *maya*—which now brings us to consider further aspects pertaining to the central focus of this book.

THE PREPARATORY 3½ YEARS
AND THE CULMINATING 3½ YEARS

As indicated in *Christ & the Maya Calendar*, Rudolf Steiner prophesied that the incarnation of Ahriman into his human vehicle would take place shortly after the year 2000.[44] Of course, it is a matter of interpretation what he meant by "shortly after." The research presented in *Christ & the Maya Calendar* concludes that "shortly after" signifies that the time-lag could be somewhere between one to two decades after 2000.

To penetrate this prophecy, we (the authors of *Christ & the Maya Calendar*) drew upon Rudolf Steiner's indications and various other sources: primarily the Book of Revelation, but also upon the prophecy concerning the coming of the Antichrist made by the American clairvoyant Jeane Dixon in her book *My Life and Prophecies* (keeping in mind, as elucidated in the table on page 31, that her reference to the *coming of the Antichrist* is to be understood as referring to the event

---

43   Azuma, "A Survey of Augmented Reality," in *Presence: Teleoperators and Virtual Environments*, August 1997, pp. 355–385.

44   "Before only a part of the third millennium of the post-Christian era has elapsed, there will be in the West an actual incarnation of Ahriman—Ahriman in the flesh." This prophetic statement relating to our time was made in a lecture on November 1, 1919—see Steiner, *The Incarnation of Ahriman*, p. 37.

prophesied by Rudolf Steiner as the *incarnation of Ahriman*). Above all, however, the astrosophical discovery of the *Apocalypse Code* was applied in *Christ & the Maya Calendar*, as it provides a precise framework for understanding the time period during which the *incarnation of Ahriman*—understood as the *coming of the Antichrist* in the Christian tradition—will take place. In light of the Apocalypse Code, this will occur during the *39th day of the temptation of humanity as a whole*, which extends from 1988 to 2018.[45] The 3½-year period of the rule of the beast indicated in chapter 13 of the Book of Revelation, commencing with the incarnation of Ahriman into his human vessel, in light of the Apocalypse code would begin not later than the year 2015, in order that the 3½ years should be completed at the latest during the year 2018.

The research presented in *Christ & the Maya Calendar* indicates the earliest possibility for this 3½-year period as dating from July 21/22, 2009 to (approximately) the end of the Maya Calendar on December 21, 2012, and the latest possibility extending from some time during the year 2015 to a point in time 3½ years later in the year 2018. At the time of writing *Christ & the Maya Calendar* (2008), the date July 21/22, 2009 was seen as a possibility for the incarnation of Ahriman, since on that date (July 21 in America, July 22 in China) there took place the longest total solar eclipse of the twenty-first century, whose path of visibility crossed India and China, where around forty percent of the world's population are living. *Christ & the Maya Calendar* was written prior to this solar eclipse. With hindsight, what can be said now, looking back at what has transpired since this event of that 2009 solar eclipse?

Looking back, *it does not appear evident* that this solar eclipse marked the time of the incarnation of Ahriman. As always, it is up to each person to ascertain independently the truth of this and other such statements made here and elsewhere, by recognizing the signs that point toward the truth, holding in consciousness the words of Christ, "By their fruits you shall know them" (Matthew 7:16). At the time of writing *Christ & the Maya Calendar*, much emphasis was

---

45 Powell, "The Apocalypse Code," *Christian Star Calendar 2009*, pp. 11–18. See also chapter 2 of *Christ & the Maya Calendar*.

placed on the longest solar eclipse of the twenty-first century in July 2009, in order to sound a clarion call—a wake-up call—regarding the imminence of the anti-Christian manifestation of the beast of Revelation, chapter 13.

According to Jeane Dixon's vision, the human vessel for the incarnation of Satan (Ahriman) was born in February 1962 on the day of a total solar eclipse. On July 21/22, 2009, marking the occurrence of the longest solar eclipse of the twenty-first century, this vessel (Mr. X) would have been forty-seven years of age. Even though it was not the time of the incarnation of Ahriman into his human vessel, it is evident that it was a time of a great influx of inspiration from Ahriman upon the Earth, particularly when viewed against the background of the various ahrimanic phenomena we have been considering in this book. Rudolf Steiner spoke of the great importance for humankind to recognize the incarnation of Ahriman—that it must not go by unnoticed, adding that it would be a tragedy for humanity if it *were* to pass by unnoticed. (He said the same, too, about the Second Coming of Christ.) To draw attention to this in relation to the current period of time, starting with the solar eclipse on July 21/22, 2009, *Christ & the Maya Calendar* was published to sound a wake-up call to readers to watch for signs of this event.

In the interest of understanding signs of the times in which we are living, the Apocalypse code looks at the life of Christ as the archetype for humanity as a whole. It postulates a time relationship between the 3½ years of Christ's life and the entire subsequent history of humankind. The key to this time relationship is that one day in the life of Christ coincides with one orbit of Saturn around the zodiac in 29½ years. According to the Apocalypse code, humankind is now undergoing collectively what Christ Jesus went through on the 39th day of the forty days in the wilderness, which is the temptation of "turning stones into bread," or the temptation of virtual reality—substituting what is not living ("virtual") in the place of creation and thereby turning stones (non-living images) into bread (giving these non-living images the appearance of being living). And virtual reality is definitely one of the keynotes of our time! As described in *Christ & the Maya Calendar*, the 39th day for humanity as a whole extends from 1988 to

2018 and it is during this 39th day that the encounter with Ahriman takes place, just as it took place on the 39th day for Christ Jesus, when Ahriman presented him with the temptation of "turning stones to bread."[46]

The next question to ask is: If July 21/22, 2009, was not the time of the emergence of the Antichrist (the incarnation of Ahriman into his human vessel, Mr. X), was it nevertheless significant in relation to some aspect of the event of Ahriman's incarnation? As will be seen in the further course of this book, the answer to this question is "yes."

> The great battle of humans with the demons has been under-way since about 1879, or even earlier—since 1841, when the Archangel Michael began to cast down the demons, the spirits of darkness. However, the culminating battle in this particular phase of the confrontation with evil began in earnest on July 22, 2009, the day of the longest solar eclipse of the twenty-first century. For this encounter, humanity is in need of spiritual wisdom and the help of higher beings, which can arise through one's longing for union with the Divine.[47]

The article from which the above quote is taken elaborates upon the large-scale infiltration of evil from the so-called *eighth sphere* into the human realm around the time of the great solar eclipse.[48] In trying to understand the July 22, 2009, eclipse date, it seems pos-sible—based on the foregoing testimony and other indications—to consider that something did begin at that time, something of extraor-dinary significance. One possible framework for comprehending the date July 22, 2009 is to consider that it bears the signature of the beginning of a *preparatory 3½-year period* leading to the *actual or culminating 3½-year period*. The preparatory period, according to

---

46 Powell, *Chronicle of the Living Christ*.

47 Frank Brown, "The Eighth Sphere," *Starlight*, newsletter of the Sophia Foundation of North America, vol. 9, no. 2 (2009), p. 22.

48 The *eighth sphere* is an esoteric term denoting a realm created by evil forces, a realm that will eventually separate from the normal evolutionary process; the closest equivalent to the *eighth sphere* in Christian terminology is indi-cated by the word *hell*. See Steiner, *The Occult Movement in the Nineteenth Century*, lectures 4 and 5.

some sources, is—like the culminating period—3½ years in length, which, when taken together with the actual 3½ years, makes a total of seven years. In this case, the preparatory period would be the 3½ years from the solar eclipse on July 21/22, 2009, to (approximately) the end of the Maya calendar on December 21, 2012—or to around January 20, 2013, if a full period of 3½ years is counted from July 21, 2009. During this preparatory period the human vessel (Mr. X) chosen for Ahriman's incarnation need not necessarily be particularly outstanding or extraordinary, as his transformation will take place only after the "baptismal event"—here drawing a parallel with the incarnation of Christ into Jesus at the baptism in the River Jordan. At this "baptismal event" the incarnation of Ahriman into his human vessel will take place. Then, according to some sources, follow the actual 3½ years spoken of in Revelation, chapter 13. These are the *culminating* 3½ years (following on from the *preparatory period*—generally also considered to be 3½ years in length). According to the astrosophical perspective offered in *Christ & the Maya Calendar,* against this background the culminating 3½ years will fall within the period (1988–2018) of the 3rd temptation, which ends in the year 2018—that is, the culminating 3½ years will fall at the latest during the period of 2015 to 2018.

It is hardly possible to be one hundred per cent certain about the exact timing of the "baptismal event," because Ahriman will choose his point of entrance onto the world stage carefully and according to many imponderables. Only then will the great transformation of the human vessel, spoken of by Daniel Andreev, will take place—followed by all the happenings and events he and others have prophesied.[49] Despite the difficulty in exactly pinpointing apocalyptic events, because of the extreme significance of this event for humanity not only did the great Austrian seer Rudolf Steiner and the American clairvoyant Jeane Dixon but also the gifted Russian

---

49 Andreev, "The Rose of the World," *Journal for Star Wisdom 2011*, p. 14: "[At a certain point in his life he will undergo a transformation.] His transformation will be noticed by people right away, yet they will not be able to recognize the meaning or the "how" [of this transformation]. The external appearance of the transformed one will remain virtually unchanged. However, a terrible and frightening energy will proceed from him."

visionary Daniel Andreev all point to the *coming of the Antichrist* (for Rudolf Steiner the *incarnation of Ahriman*) out of their spiritual faculties, confirming what is prophesied in Revelation, chapter 13, where the *beast* is referred to (meaning the *incarnation of Ahriman*). At the time of writing *Christ & the Maya Calendar*, I did not have access to the lengthy description by Daniel Andreev of his visions of the coming of the Antichrist. As Daniel Andreev's account of this event is by far the most extensive—devoting some two hundred pages to discussing this in the latter half of his magnum opus, *The Rose of the World,* only the first half of which has been published in English translation[50]—it was not possible at that time to include the perspective offered by this great Russian seer and poet. This book/update is intended to rectify this omission. A start with this rectification began in the 2011 issue of the *Journal for Star Wisdom*, where part of Daniel Andreev's vision of the coming of the Antilogos was published for the first time in English translation (see appendix 1). Daniel Andreev's contribution enables us to understand Rudolf Steiner's prophecy of "the beast who will rise up in 1933" in a new light having to do with the emergence in 1933 of two human beings from the *school of Ahriman* onto the world stage, as discussed in the following.

Jeane Dixon's vision is discussed in this book's introduction, where it is mentioned that the leading pioneer of astrosophy, Willi Sucher, affirmed the accuracy of the date of her vision. Given that Jeane Dixon was very specific about the birth date (February 5, 1962) of the human vessel for the incarnation of Ahriman, and given the perspective of the Apocalypse code, one can be fairly certain, as already indicated, that the culminating 3½ years will lie within the present period of the Apocalypse code, ending in the year 2018, as discussed in *Christ & the Maya Calendar*.[51] And if the preparatory years really do coincide with the period from the solar eclipse on July 21/22, 2009, to the end of the Maya calendar, then the culminating 3½ years might

---

50 Andreev, *The Rose of the World*. This volume contains in English translation the first half of the Russian original, entitled *Rosa Mira*.

51 If the human vessel for the incarnation of Ahriman was born on February 5, 1962, this human being will be fifty-six in 2018.

indeed commence around the December 21, 2012, Maya calendar date, as implied in the sub-title of *Christ & the Maya Calendar*—or they might begin around January 20, 2013, as mentioned already, if the full period of 3½ years is counted from July 21/22, 2009. In other words, the "baptismal event" of the incarnation of Ahriman might be around December 21, 2012, or one month later, around January 20, 2013—at least, this can be treated as a working hypothesis.

The time in which we are presently living is known as the *age of the consciousness soul*,[52] which means the age of awakening consciously to the reality of the Spirit. It is during this time that the Mystery of Evil is being unveiled, just as in the previous age the Mystery of Death was the primary theme.[53] In the previous epoch (747 BC–AD 1414), known as the *age of the mind (or intellectual) soul*, the Mystery of Death was illuminated by Christ's resurrection—his overcoming death. The Words of Christ that would express this, if such were to have been spoken to the disciples by the Risen One after his resurrection, could be formulated along these lines: *The heavenly Father sent me to overcome death. I have triumphed over death. For, behold, I have risen from the tomb as the first-born of the dead. As the Risen One I show you the path for all humanity into the future.* Likewise, in the present great struggle with evil, when the Antichrist (the incarnated Satan or Ahriman) is overcome, as described in the section toward the end of this book entitled "Future Perspectives," corresponding words by Christ that would express this future event

---

52 In Rudolf Steiner's description of spiritual evolution, successive periods of 2,160 years corresponding to the signs of the zodiac unfold historically. He called these periods *cultural epochs*. He described the *age of the consciousness soul* as the fifth cultural epoch since the destruction of Atlantis through the great flood and dated this current fifth epoch, corresponding to the Age of Pisces, from the year 1413/1414 to 3573/3574. As described in Powell & Dann, *The Astrological Revolution*, the Age of Pisces lasts 2,160 years, from AD 215 to 2375, and the corresponding cultural epoch, the age of the consciousness soul, began in 1414—after a time-lag of 1,199 years—almost 1,200 years after the start of the Age of Pisces, where the time-lag of 1,199 years is an astronomical period associated with the planet Venus, comprising two 600-year cultural waves. According to Steiner, a cultural wave lasts for six hundred years, whereas a cultural epoch lasts for 2,160 years.

53 Rudolf Steiner, *From the History & Contents of the First Section of the Esoteric School 1904–1914* (Complete Works, vol. 264—Great Barrington/MA: SteinerBooks, 2010), Introduction.

could be formulated as follows: *The heavenly Father sent me to overcome evil. I have triumphed over evil. For, behold, I have cast down the evil one. As the Power of the Good, the source for the Good to prevail, I show you the path for all humanity into the future.*

A wake-up call is needed if human beings are to align themselves consciously with Christ in the confrontation between Good and Evil, and that is the endeavor of this book, just as it has been the purpose of the book *Christ & the Maya Calendar.*

✝

In the introduction, we compared the horoscope of Stalin's death with the horoscope of the February 5, 1962, birth of the Antichrist (Mr. X), the human vessel for the incarnation of Ahriman according to Jeane Dixon's vision. On the basis of this horoscope comparison, it emerges in the introduction that there is an exact fulfillment of the second rule of astrological reincarnation, and that there are also occurrences of several other planetary alignments between the two horoscopes. Thus, astrosophical evidence is provided in support of the feasibility of the hypothesis that the reincarnated Stalin was born as Mr. X on February 5, 1962, and that consequently February 5, 2012 is the fiftieth birthday of this individuality. While this astrosophical finding does not prove the hypothesis, it lends support to it.

Now let us consider the question of the authenticity of Jeane Dixon's vision upon which the forgoing hypothesis rests. Victor Zelikovsky considers the prophetic vision seen by Jeane Dixon of the birth on February 5, 1962, to be authentic, although he does not consider the "end-time dates" (the years immediately following 1999) indicated by Jeane Dixon to be accurate, but rather, he focuses upon the end of the Maya calendar in December 2012 "as a constant warning of the urgency of the time."[54] After commenting on the technical

---

54 Zelikovsky, *2012: Prophecies of the Emerging Golden Age,* p. 38. Victor Zelikovsky (Tibor Zelikovics) was born in Hungary in 1948, emigrating with his family to the United States in 1956. He studied philosophy and political science at the University of California, Berkeley and UCLA; Old Testament theology at the Yeshiva Hebrew Academy in New Haven, Connecticut. Residing in Europe since 1971, he is cofounder and director of the Vienna Metaphysical Society as well as president of the Metaphysical Society of Switzerland.

structure of the global surveillance system, in his discussion of the Antichrist (*the incarnated Ahriman* in the words of Rudolf Steiner) taking over the global infrastructure, he writes:

> The Antichrist will probably come to terms with the big multinational corporations (or they with him) and maintain their logistic organizations to ensure a smoothly functioning global infrastructure. Another way of seeing the picture is to consider that a close cooperation probably already exists between the Antichrist and the powers behind the major international commercial

Joseph Stalin as a young man

and financial institutions, who presently appear to be, efficiently and decidedly, preparing the way for the coming world government.[55]

The purpose of this whole book is to create a framework in which readers will be able to come—in freedom, through inner knowing—to their own conclusion concerning the identity of the human vessel for the incarnation of Ahriman. As already mentioned, according to Rudolf Steiner this conclusion/cognition will be of vital significance for the evolution of the Earth and humanity. What to do, then, with this cognition, if—through grace—the truth is revealed to one, which it should be, if Rudolf Steiner is to be taken seriously? It is easy to imagine that initially there may be a sense of betrayal—even anger or hatred—and also fear. Consciously penetrating through the veil of ahrimanic *maya* and—as one could imagine—coming to a perception

---

55   Ibid., p. 202.

of blatant lying, deception, cynicism, and behind-the-scenes manipulation, what could one say or do?

One could have compassion for Mr. X as a "Judas of the Etheric Christ," who no doubt will play the role scripted for him, and who probably will not even know—at least, not fully consciously—that he is a servant of evil. Like Judas two thousand years ago, this "Judas of the Etheric Christ"—this soul who perhaps long ago was a radiant light, but who in the course of his more recent incarnations since the time of Christ has fallen—whose messianic qualities have been so well described by Jeane Dixon—will probably be hopelessly in the clutches of ahrimanic forces. His role will be to serve as an external manifestation of the *double of humankind*, at this time of humanity's crossing the threshold in the great initiation trial leading to conscious awareness of Christ in the etheric realm.[56] Knowing this, an appropriate response is to focus one's efforts upon preparing for the encounter with the Etheric Christ, and to participate in the work of Christ and Sophia in bringing to birth the new culture known as the *Rose of the World*, as a culture based on Divine Love and Wisdom—this being the answer in terms of the Divine Plan to the decadent and corrupt ahrimanic culture of our time.

As described in the introduction, the *modus operandi* of Mr. X as a "Judas of the Etheric Christ" is deception on a grand scale, including deceiving the public with regard to his date of birth. Let us reflect upon the "why" and the "how" of the concealing of the true date of birth. The "why" is clear: If this person came to power and it was known that he was born on February 5, 1962, he would immediately be identified as the human being referred to in Jeane Dixon's vision, in which her communication of this date as the date of birth of the vessel for the incarnation of Satan (Ahriman), whom she refers to as the Antichrist, is given.

The "how" is more complex. Obviously, if the true date of birth of Mr. X is February 5, 1962, then the assumed (the false date of birth) cannot be too far removed from this date—otherwise, in terms of age and appearance, the fictitious date of birth would not be plau-

---

56   See my two articles: "In Memory of Willi Sucher" and "World Pentecost" in the *Journal for Star Wisdom 2010* for the context of this initiation trial.

sible. The deeper issue raised here, though, is this: Is it conceivable in today's highly bureaucratic world that someone could come to power having a forged birth certificate showing a false date of birth? There is no easy answer to this question. All that can be said is that such a birth—and also the conception, which probably would have taken place in May 1961—would most likely have been the subject of a certain degree of intrigue, given the interest of Ahriman himself in shepherding the incarnation of his chosen vessel.

Because of this, it is possible that not only the date of birth but also the place of birth might be falsified. Jeane Dixon did not give a specific location as the birth place of this human being but indicated that she saw him "born of humble peasant origin" at a location somewhere "in the Middle East"—thus denoting the child in her vision as the *Child of the East*. As referred to in the article "In Memory of Willi Sucher" in the 2010 issue of the *Journal for Star Wisdom*, Willi Sucher affirmed on the basis of his own research that Jeane Dixon's vision was accurate with regard to the date of birth of the vessel for Ahriman's incarnation, but that he saw the place of birth not in the Middle East but in Africa—more specifically, he referred to Tobruk, Libya, as the place of birth of the human vessel for Ahriman's incarnation. However, given the current political climate, it is difficult to envision someone from the Middle East, let alone from Libya, ascending to the peak of world power. Whether born in the Middle East or elsewhere, the necessity of faking the place of birth of the "world emperor" also emerges as a strong possibility in addition to the falsification of the date of his birth.

According to the prophecy of Daniel Andreev, an elite oligarchy brings Mr. X to power as the "world emperor." Based on his past performance in the previous incarnation as Stalin, the elite, as members of the ruling oligarchy, could well become the victims of show trials or even extrajudicial execution, if perceived to be in any way opposed to Mr. X, just as Stalin ruthlessly persecuted members of the Politburo whom he suspected of not being completely aligned with him, or whom he simply did not like.

FUTURE PERSPECTIVES

Much more could be said along the lines of our previous consider-ations. The purpose of bringing these considerations is not to awaken fear of what is coming, but to prepare humanity for a great trial—one that according to Revelation 13 is foreseen in humankind's spiritual evolution and has a definite significance. In the space of this book it is not possible to go into the deeper significance of this trial, which is discussed at length in the book *Christ & the Maya Calendar*. It suffices to say that "forewarned is forearmed." As already mentioned, we are living in the age of the consciousness soul, which entails *being conscious*. To be conscious means taking a sober look at the actual state of affairs in the world, difficult though this may be, and articu-lating our cognitions of the facts that we perceive.[57] This is a first step. A next step is to inwardly offer up our cognitions to the spiri-tual world in a prayerful way, asking for help and guidance. "Ask and you shall receive," is how Christ Jesus expressed it—he who is "the way, *the truth*, and the life." The most important point here is to hold in consciousness the context for this encounter with the incar-nated Ahriman, as a trial for humanity leading to the meeting with Christ in his Second Coming, as described in the two articles "In Memory of Willi Sucher" and "World Pentecost" in *Journal for Star Wisdom 2010* (see appendix 3).

As expressed at the outset of this book, it is important to be *spiritually armed* (in the sense of St. Paul's words to the Ephesians quoted on page 29) in order to emerge victorious from the trial of the encounter with the Antichrist (the incarnated Ahriman), "to quench the flaming arrows of the evil one" (from the quote by Paul). Knowledge of this trial is essential as a first step—this being the main purpose of this book. Second, it is of paramount importance to align oneself with Christ, who taught these words from the Lord's prayer, "Deliver us from evil" ultimately signifying "Deliver us from the evil

---

57 A wonderful example of this is presented in the recent book by Prince Charles: *Harmony: A New Way of Looking at Our World*. It takes a sober look at the crisis threatening our whole civilization because of our discon-nection from nature and offers practical guidance as to how balance and harmony between humanity and nature can be restored.

one,"[58] relating to the encounter with the incarnated Ahriman as the personification of evil. These words are a powerful mantra, given by Christ for this situation. Together with the other words of the Lord's prayer,[59] they offer a key to the initiation trial of the encounter with Ahriman. The successful passage through this trial will signify, *while still remaining sovereign on the physical plane of existence*, that an ongoing relationship is established with the new realm of spiritual experience into which Christ—who, in his Second Coming, is already within the etheric realm—is leading human beings.

The context for this trial, let us always remember, is the event of Christ's Second Coming. In the words of Daniel Andreev:

> [After the death of Mr. X, the vessel for the incarnated Ahriman, who is referred to by Daniel Andreev as the Antichrist] the world state rapidly collapses and it is only through drastic measures that anarchy in various parts of the world is hindered.... "And there appears a great sign in heaven: a woman clothed with the Sun...." [Revelation 12:1]. Who is the *woman clothed with the Sun*? It is *Zventa-Sventana* [Sophia], embraced by the Planetary

---

58   *Deliver us from the evil one* is the translation offered by the New International Version of the Bible (2011).

59   *Deliver us from evil* are the closing words of the Lord's prayer as spoken by Christ Jesus, as recorded in the Gospel of St. Matthew. In the early Christian centuries the words *For thine is the kingdom and the power and the glory, for ever and ever. Amen* were added as closing words to the Lord's prayer. These words are not found in the earliest versions of the Matthew Gospel. The first reference—albeit abbreviated to: *For thine is the power and the glory for ever*—is in the *Teaching of the Twelve Apostles* (8:1), written shortly after AD 100. In a complete form, these words are subsequently found in the second (or third) century Syriac *Peshitta* Bible—James Murdock, *The Syriac New Testament*, p. 9. How did these words come to be added to the Lord's prayer? It is not generally known that they were inspired by the Risen One himself. Deeper study and contemplation reveals that these closing words were communicated by the Risen One as a prophetic announcement of his Second Coming and are a powerful means of connecting with the *Parousia*, the Divine Presence of Christ in his Second Coming. It is significant that these words follow directly after *Deliver us from the evil one* relating to the encounter with incarnated Ahriman as the personification of evil. The words *For thine is the kingdom and the power and the glory, for ever and ever. Amen* were given to us by the Risen Christ as the "light at the end of the tunnel" guiding us through the initiation trial of this encounter with the evil one expressed in the words *Deliver us from the evil one.*

Logos and chosen to give birth to the Great Spirit of the Second Aeon. The mirroring of this event in world history is the *Rose of the World,* whose utmost striving before, during, and after the time of the Antichrist prepares humanity to become a vessel for the Great Spirit....[60]

The wedding feast begins. The Planetary Logos and the Planetary Church are united in unspeakable love....The Second Aeon, spoken of by the prophets as a thousand-year kingdom of the righteous, starts. Its goal is the salvation of all, without exception, regardless as to how low they fell, how far they have remained behind, or how deeply entrenched they may be in the realms of purgatory. The goal is the transformation of *Shadanakar* [comprising the spiritual, soul, ethereal, and physical levels of the Earth] in its entirety.... Earth's divine humanity, those led by Christ and *Zventa-Sventana* [Sophia], are no longer to be separated from them.[61] They will commence with the reshaping of their predecessors on *Enrof* [the physical Earth and in an extended sense the physical level of existence] and with the spiritualization of suffering nature as well as of the cities of the world. The Second Aeon will be a time where there is no longer any physical birth for human beings, no illness, no pain, no fighting or hatred. There will be Love and Creativity, in order to redeem the "departed ones" and to illumine all layers of matter.... Only the Omniscient One knows how many millennia the kingdom of the righteous should last on the Earth. Time itself will go through a metamorphosis. Time will resound as a golden symphony of streams of time running parallel to one another. There will no longer be what we today call *history.* Not history, but [rather] the

---

60   Andrejew, *Rosa Mira,* vol. 3, pp. 202–225. For the context of these words, see Andreev, "The Rose of the World," *Journal for Star Wisdom 2011;* see also appendix 1.

61   RP: In the Book of Revelation, Christ and Sophia are referred to as the Lamb and his Bride. These words communicated by Daniel Andreev indicate that those human beings who attain a certain level of union with Christ and Sophia are then inseparable from them. This is the ultimate goal for humanity. The attainment of this level of union with the Lamb and his Bride— Divine Love and Divine Wisdom—is, in the last analysis, the protection against demonic possession as exemplified in the case of individuals such as Hitler and Stalin.

growth—ever-increasing—of universal harmony will be the content of time.[62]

An unimaginable jubilation takes hold of this and other worlds, and humanity passes through a great, light-filled transformation. The prince of darkness will terrify human beings.... Christ, however, will take on as many forms as there are consciousnesses on Earth to behold him. He will adapt himself to everyone, and will converse with all. His forms, in an unimaginable way, will simultaneously yield an image: *One who appears in heaven surrounded by unspeakable glory.* There will not be a single being on Earth who will not see the Son of God and hear his Word....[63]

The Second Coming is to occur simultaneously at a multitude of points on [Earth]...so that every single being will have seen and heard Him. In other words, the Planetary Logos is to attain the inconceivable power to materialize simultaneously in as many places as there will then be consciousness to perceive Him...so that all peoples and nations on Earth will see "the Son of Man coming on the clouds of heaven."[64]

These words by Daniel Andreev are of a prophetic nature, written shortly before his death in 1959. Now, over fifty years later, not only the encounter with the Son of Man but also the hearing of his Word is possible. At the present time, it is this meeting with the Son of Man as he can now be experienced, which is the most important event that anyone in earthly existence can undergo. This is the spiritual event that is the initiatory aspect for human beings of humanity's encounter with the incarnated Ahriman.

As an example of this spiritual event, consider this account of a young woman, Estelle Isaacson, of her initiatory experience of Christ through the Mystery of Golgotha.[65] The following description of her

---

62 Ibid., pp. 225–229. Translated from the German by RP and published here in English translation for the first time.

63 Ibid., pp. 225–226. Translated from the German by RP. For the context of these words, see Daniel Andreev, "The Rose of the World," *Journal for Star Wisdom 2011*, p. 15; see also appendix 1.

64 Andreev, *The Rose of the World*, p. 342.

65 Estelle Isaacson, a young woman who has until now contributed anonymously to the *Journal for Star Wisdom*, is an example of a contemporary

meeting with Christ, which took place on February 18, 2011, can be a source of inspiration to everyone.

In this description the relationship of Christ to the *Central Sun* emerges. Appendix I in *Christ & the Maya Calendar* is about the Central Sun as the Divine Heart of our Milky Way galaxy—known in astronomy as the *galactic center*. From this Divine Heart, two mediating Divine Essences emanate: Divine Love (Christ) and Divine Wisdom (Sophia). As described in appendix 1 of *Christ & the Maya Calendar*, the Central Sun is the place of origin of both Christ and Sophia. Long ago Christ (Divine Love) descended from the Central Sun upon the lengthy path of incarnation, which culminated two thousand years ago at the baptism in the River Jordan in his union with the human being Jesus of Nazareth, and now Divine Wisdom (Sophia) is on a long and gradual path of descent from the Central Sun, a path of incarnation to unite with our Sun around the year 2375, the start of the Age of Aquarius, which could thus also be called the Age of Sophia.[66] Sophia's path of incarnation follows that taken by Christ who, with his incarnation, inaugurated a *new aeon* of time for humankind and the Earth. Christ—for the first time in the history of the Earth—brought down the power of the Central Sun, which is Divine Love, for the transformation of the Earth and humanity into the *new earth* of the Book of Revelation. Now Sophia is on a similar path of incarnation, originating from the Central Sun, to bring Divine Wisdom (the *new heaven* of Revelation) to humanity and the Earth, whereby her union with our Sun at the start of the Age of Aquarius will be one stage on her journey, which will be followed by further stages, drawing ever nearer to humanity and the Earth, culminating with the founding of the *Rose of the World* as a new global culture based on Love and Wisdom. According to Daniel Andreev, the coming of Sophia will inaugurate the *second aeon*.

---

mystic, who has had several experiences of Christ in the etheric realm. See also the article by Isaacson and the article about her, published in the Easter 2011 issue of *Starlight*, the newsletter of the Sophia Foundation of North America; free download: **http://sophiafoundation.org/newsletter/**

66 Powell, "Sophia and the Rose of the World"; http://sophiafoundation.org/articles/

Second, reference is also made in the following description to Shambhala. Originating in the Tibetan Buddhist tradition, there are various meanings ascribed to Shambhala, the primary one being that it is hidden land—for some, physical, for others, non-physical—accessible only to highly evolved individuals. Rudolf Steiner gave this expression a specific meaning as the *golden heart of the Earth*. This is the region to which Christ descended after his death on the cross. From Shambhala he then ascended as the Risen One. Hence the immense importance of Shambhala in Christian esotericism, as a place of Eternal Life, whence the force for the resurrection of the body is drawn.[67]

Here, now, is Estelle Isaacson's account of her initiatory experience of Christ through the Mystery of Golgotha. This account is so profound and offers such a level of attunement to the Etheric Christ that it can be read several times, and it is most effective if read aloud—best of all in a group, in the spirit of the words: "Where two or three are gathered in my name, there am I in your midst" (Matthew 18:20).

This vision, which Estelle Isaacson had on February 18, 2011, offers a message of hope to the world at this time, as does her vision of September 11, 2009 (see pages 88–90).

⭒

THE DIVINE HARMONIES OF THE BLOOD OF CHRIST

I again traversed the boundary of time and found myself at the foot of the Cross; He beheld me, His bruised and bleeding head bowed over me. A drop of His precious Blood fell from His forehead onto mine as He continued to behold me. I felt His life enter into me where His Blood touched my forehead, planting the seed of Himself within me. *His Blood is so precious!* I felt at one with the Earth that was receiving His Blood beneath the Cross—I deepened into the Earth's perspective and experienced how it was for the Earth to receive Him, as she took in His great drops of Blood:

---

67 For the source of Rudolf Steiner's designation of Shambhala as the *golden heart of the Earth*, and concerning the relationship of Shambhala to the interior of the Earth, see Powell, "Subnature and the Second Coming," in *The Inner Life of the Earth*, pp. 69–141.

Such divine order in His Blood! So divine, and yet at the same time, so human! I heard the harmonies in His Blood—the sound of the divine merging with the human—the tones of this merging! Everywhere His Blood touched the Earth, the Earth opened etherically, rising up to meet Him, becoming a chalice, resounding with a great *"Ah!"* I could feel this within my own self—my soul becoming a chalice to receive, carved out through immense suffering. *Holy, Holy Lord! Your beauty is so unspeakable!*

My eyes never left Him as He died. I remained with Him fully present in His death, beholding Him for quite some time, just wanting to contemplate His body in silence. It seemed as if I was the only one there with His body, and was given all the time that I wanted to be with Him. My soul cried out in agony for what they had done to the Christ! As I was thus in contemplation, feeling the pain of the burning flame in my forehead where His Blood had fallen, I suddenly felt Him alight upon me, as if a huge mystical bird settled upon me, then descending into me, unfolding its wings, filling every measure of my own being, and then passing through me into the Earth.

I then witnessed His descent from the Cross, the Blessed Mother holding His body in her arms and the other Marys and John each had a hand on Him while they grieved. Time stood still. What happened next is almost impossible to relay, but I will attempt.

FROM THE CENTRAL SUN TO SHAMBHALA

I again saw Christ on the Cross, only this time it was as if the Cross was hovering in a tremendous amount of light; I was hearing the merging of the divine and human tones of His Blood together—the earthly and the heavenly commingling in His Blood. I was at one with His Blood. As His Blood fell, again the Earth became a chalice— and His Blood mingling with the Earth resounded as if the chalice of the Earth became a singing bowl—sending this resonance out into the Universe, all the way to the Central Sun! And the Central Sun, which then appeared in resplendent view behind the Cross, reflected this resonance back to the Earth with all of its divine tones; I was between Heaven and Earth hearing the conversation of divine and earthly harmonies weaving back and forth between the Central Sun and the Earth while Christ's Blood fell into the Earth! It was as if the tones were answering each other in seraphic symphony, in consummate supernal order. Beethoven's 9th symphony came to my mind as being the best earthly representation of these harmonies.

With incredulity I was given to understand that the tones that were woven between heaven and Earth are *still present*. I saw the harmonies stretch out into the cosmos like a highway of light. These harmonies are the way by which we may travel—*the narrow way to eternal life!* The bridge between the worlds! These are the very tones and codes of life itself! The seed of Abraham, the sands without number; numberless worlds reside within this narrow way. Difficult to find, and once found, it is just as difficult to remain. The delicate web the spider spins—so hard to see, so tiny, yet so strong. If you can find the Way and hold to it, it will open to you. I could never profess to be fully there, yet I yearn for it with my entire soul.

The Cross disappeared and Christ was hovering above me, gazing into my eyes as He spoke the words: *It is fulfilled*. These words coursed through the cosmos, harmonizing with the Central Sun and then returning to resound with the Earth. This was absolutely indescribable! The light of the Central Sun flowed through His eyes and His words and His light entered completely into my being. And I rose and held to His feet, feeling an incredible power flow from His feet into my hands—and then He passed through me like a great mystical bird.

His blood in the Earth is eternal. We can know Him through the Earth. He gave the gift of His Blood to the Earth.

While seeing the vision of His Blood falling to the Earth, I also received simultaneously a vision of His conception—again, this was the commingling of the divine and the human. I saw Mary, taken up and the seed from the Central Sun planted within her. I experienced the harmonies in her—the harmonies of the Immaculate Conception of Jesus Christ, as she gave her human blood to Him. There is so much in this miracle that cannot be spoken.

His Blood on my forehead—like the tear-dropped shape of the flame of Pentecost—burned throughout my being. Joyous and awe-struck, I saw the Earth enveloped in the light of the Father's presence from the Central Sun, being held in the Father's embrace. My soul felt a surge of strength, uniting me more fully than ever before with the Earth, feeling a tremendous love for the Earth, along with a solid knowing that it is destiny that I am on Earth at this time. In that moment of awakening, the sword of Michael pierced me through the center of my being all the way to the center of the Earth, to Shambhala. I felt a strength within me I had never felt before—a strength in being fully connected to the Earth. I experienced the Earth like His wound; the nail that pierced His hand is like the sword of Michael piercing the Earth, and the sword that pierced Mary's heart. We must be pierced also so that the Divine can mingle with us. I felt such strength being the one that pierces and the one that is pierced, the Earth receiving me and I receiving the strength of Shambhala. *Thank you, Dear Lord! The Lord is my strength!* I now see the sword through the center of my being inscribed with His Word and His Word is my strength! His Word resonates and reverberates from the sword within me. Incredible love and warmth radiated from the sword within me—such strength and peace! *Be it unto me according to thy will.*

I know that I must have a strong presence in the Earth; I must not allow fear to pull me away from the Earth; I cannot serve Her if I leave Her. It is time for me to be strongly present, so that the strength of the Lord can penetrate the Earth through my willingness to remain. I am not the one who gives life to the Earth. I know the One who gives life and I am a conduit for the One, He who is the Light that comes to Earth and touches us with His Love. I thank the Lord that there are others who are doing this work—we are all connected through His body bringing His Light to the world who receives us with awe. And when we are still, having calmed the inner storms, we can hear the resonating of the *"Ah!"* of the Earth meeting the *"Ah!"* of the Divine as whispers in our souls.

[Christ spoke these words:]

Be still and know that I AM God in you. For your very cells are chalices that receive Me. Oh precious child of the Earth, you are a Child of Light. I have sent you to Earth imprinted with divine memory. The Earth receives you and calls you Her own. The seed of Christ is within you and as the seed awakens within you, you shall find others in whom the seed is awakening also. You are the Sons and Daughters of Light, living seeds, sustenance of the Earth, sustenance that will lift humanity and carry it through the dark times; for the seeds of destruction are being plunged into the Earth!

Child of Light!

You are the answer, the antidote! Everything is in your divine memory, all the codes are housed within you—you are the hope for future generations. Indeed the future generations have placed you here to prepare for those who will redeem the Earth, and you shall come again in the future. You are planting the seeds for your own futures and shall come again to carry this work forward. You are heralds bearing the message of Christ for this time frame. And the spiritual worlds bear record of you and stand in awe of you; the record that they bear will bless the generations hereafter. The divine memory is imprinted in your very DNA; you can draw from this wellspring. Call upon the sacred magic that you carry within you to bless the Earth, to sanctify Nature. This wellspring reaches all the way to Shambhala, a never-ending source for you. Exercise wisdom as you reach down into this spring for you shall be given challenges, lessons, and shall suffer through temptations in order to prepare you, to try you, until you are ready to utilize these sacred powers—even the sacred powers of Shambhala. You will fall in the process. Have no fear. It is a time of learning. You will go through the pain and suffering until you are as pure as glass. This is the journey you are already on. Have faith in yourself. When you fall, repent and move on. Continue forward.

Always hold the Earth in the center of your chalice, your soul, which is being carved to ever greater breadths and depths by your suffering, which gives you greater capacity to hold the Earth in pure Love, and to know what you can do to bless the Earth through these dark times.

Inwardly strive to always be in a state of rest, which means having faith. Be like the infant who easily sleeps in the safety of her mother's arms. She has faith in her mother, for her mother is always concerned for her and is always loving her; she knows she will receive nourishment when she needs it, and is always protected. And so her mind is at rest. Know this, Child of Light, and have faith that your Divine Mother is holding you now and She will feed you and will never leave you, and Her love has no end. Take strength in knowing this and allow your mind to rest. This will allow the angels to work through you, for they cannot if your mind is in a state of fear. Rest, O Child of Light, in the bosom of the Mother! Receive Her Light and sustenance into your being.

Peace, Peace, Peace! Hear the AUM resonating from Her heart to yours.

And so it is. Amen.

✝

POSTSCRIPT

As a postscript, the recently published book *Descent into the Depths of the Earth* by Judith von Halle (cited on page 8) offers important new spiritual material concerning Sorath, who is discussed in *Christ & the Maya Calendar,* chapters 7 and 8, as well as in this book (see table on page 31). Sorath is identical to the "two-horned beast" referred to in Revelation 13:13: "[The two-horned beast] performed great and miraculous signs, even causing fire to come down from heaven to Earth in full view of men." In the discussion earlier in this book concerning the possible meaning of these words in our time, the question was raised: Could it be that these prophetic words from Revelation are coming to realization in our time, now that it is possible to cause artificial bolts of lightning through laser technology (akin to lightning) to come down from the atmosphere "in full view of men"? The answer is in the affirmative. A key year is 1998, which is three times 666, the number associated with Sorath. *Christ & the Maya Calendar* referred to 1998 as the possible time when the two-horned beast, the false prophet, whose number is 666, would emerge. Furthermore, it seems likely that this reference pertains to the activation, beginning in the 1990s, of sophisticated high-tech weaponry using advanced laser technology.[68]

Whereas this book focuses more upon the shadow side of Christ's Second Coming—the coming of the Antichrist (the incarnation of Ahriman)—my article "2012: Prophecy—Phenomena—Hope" in the *Journal for Star Wisdom 2012* focuses on the event of the Second Coming: the reappearance of Christ in the etheric realm.[69]

---

68 See, for example, www.forbiddenknowledgetv.com/page/464.html and www.agriculturedefensecoalition.org/?q=haarp-and-hipas.

69 See also my article "The Mystery of Christ in our Time" for further elucidation concerning the Etheric Christ as the *Parousia*, the Presence of Christ in the etheric realm in our time: https://sophiafoundation.org/articles/.

Appendix I
The Rose of the World (*Rosa Mira*)
by Daniel Andreev

By warning about the coming Antichrist, and pointing him out and unmasking him when he appears, by cultivating unshakable faith within human hearts and a grasp of the meta-historical perspectives and global spiritual prospects within human minds...[we help Sophia bring to birth the new culture of love and wisdom called by Daniel Andreev the "Rose of the World"]...[Sophia's] birth in one of the *zatomis* will be mirrored not only by the Rose of the World. Feminine power and its role in contemporary life is increasing everywhere. It is that circumstance above all that is giving rise to worldwide peace movements, an abhorrence of bloodshed, disillusion over coercive methods of change, an increase in woman's role in society proper, an ever-growing tenderness and concern for children, and a burning hunger for beauty and love. We are entering an age when the female soul will become ever purer and broader, when an ever greater number of women will become profound inspirers, sensitive mothers, wise counselors and far-sighted leaders. It will be an age when the feminine in humanity will manifest itself with unprecedented strength, striking a perfect balance with masculine impulses. See, you who have eyes.[1]

The words quoted are those of Daniel Andreev, the great prophet of the coming Age of Sophia and the corresponding Sophianic culture that he called the "Rose of the World." In the above quote, "zatomis" refers to a heavenly realm within the Earth's etheric aura. Andreev refers to Sophia as "Zventa-Sventana," meaning "the Holiest of the Holy."

---

1   Daniel Andreev, *The Rose of the World*, p. 358 [words in brackets in quotations added by Robert Powell].

A mysterious event is taking place in the meta-history of contemporary times: new divine-creative energy is emanating into our cosmos. Since ancient times the loftiest hearts and most subtle minds have anticipated this event that is now taking place. The first link in the chain of events—events so important that they can only be compared to the incarnation of the Logos—occurred at the turn of the nineteenth century. This was an emanation of the energy of the Virgin Mother, an emanation that was not amorphous, as it had been before in human history [at Pentecost, when there was an emanation of Sophia into the Virgin Mary], but incomparably intensified by the personal aspect it assumed. A great God-born monad descended from the heights of the universe into our cosmos.[2]

The words of the great Russian seer, Daniel Andreev, are prophetic. As indicated in *The Most Holy Trinosophia and the New Revelation of the Divine Feminine*, he points to the descent of Sophia and the resulting Sophianic world culture, the Rose of the World, in a most inspiring way:

She is to be born in a body of enlightened ether.... There She is, our hope and joy, Light and Divine Beauty! For Her birth will be mirrored in our history as something that our grandchildren and great-grandchildren will witness: the founding of the Rose of the World, its spread throughout the world, and...the assumption by the Rose of the World of supreme authority over the entire Earth.[3]

The Sophia Foundation of North America was founded and exists to help usher in the new Age of Sophia and the corresponding Sophianic culture—the Rose of the World prophesied by Daniel Andreev and other spiritual teachers.

As quoted at the beginning, "Warning about the coming Antichrist, and pointing him out and unmasking him when he appears..." is important. As discussed in the article "In Memory of Willi Sucher" in *Journal for Star Wisdom 2010*,

---

2   Ibid., p. 356.

3   Ibid., p. 357.

Humanity's encounter with the Antichrist is part of the initiation trial of humanity as a whole crossing the threshold. The external aspect of this initiation trial is the meeting with the Antichrist as the embodiment of the sum-total of humanity's negative karma, *the double of humankind as a whole*. The inner aspect is the encounter with Christ or the Archangel Michael as the Guardian of the Threshold. The result of successfully passing through this initiation trial is the opening up of conscious awareness of the angelic realm. This is one aspect of the great event at the culmination of the process of humankind as a whole crossing the threshold. Another aspect of this culmination is depicted in the article on World Pentecost.

More than anyone else, Daniel Andreev, as prophet of the coming Sophia culture, the Rose of the World, had a visionary experience of the coming of the Antichrist. His words concerning this are not to be found in the English edition of the *Rose of the World*. Because of the importance of Daniel Andreev's vision of the coming of the Antichrist, his words about this are published here for the first time in English translation.

The German translation of Daniel Andreev's *Rosa Mira: Rose of the World* (three volumes) comprises a translation of the *whole* of the original Russian text, whereas the English edition published by Lindisfarne Books represents only to the first of the three German volumes. The following translation from German is by Robert Powell, with remarks in brackets [ ] added by him for the sake of clarification. It is from volume three, pages 202 to 226.

✝

The Preparation of Human Beings for the Coming Antilogos

Certainly, humanity has not lacked warnings. Not only the *New Testament* but also the *Koran* and even the *Mahabharata* have warned us in the distant past. Haven't spiritual seers in the East and in the West proclaimed the Antichrist as an unavoidable evil? All leaders of the Rose of the World will concentrate their forces upon the work of warning about this monster.... This bearer of a dark mission will probably not really grasp whom he serves and for whom he prepares the way. For, with all his intellectual genius, his mind will be completely closed to anything of a mystical nature.... He will be greeted enthusiastically: "There he is! The one we have been waiting for...." Only much later, when the "savior" holds the entire power in his hands, will he show his true force.... Is it a matter of a human being? Yes and no. On several occasions [in *Rosa Mira*] I have indicated that this individual was incarnated as a Roman emperor and how he over the centuries, from life to life, became enveloped in demonic substance. Concerning this monad, whom Gagtungr [Ahriman/Satan] himself has kidnapped...already enough has been said about his previous incarnation [as Stalin] in Russia.... [In that incarnation] the forces of providence hindered [the attempt of Satan] to make of him a dark, universal genius. [Now, 1958, he is being prepared] for the successful carrying out of the historic role of the Antichrist. Stalin's tyrannical genius and his ability to hypnotically control the will of others is well known.... [When he reincarnates as the Antichrist] he will have at his disposal an enormous capacity for work and a multitude of talents.... He will be uniquely and terribly beautiful. From his facial characteristics it will be difficult to place him in any particular race or nation. Rather, he will be seen as a representative of the collective of humanity.... [At a certain point in his life he will undergo a transformation.] His transformation will be noticed by people right away, yet they will not be able to recognize the meaning or the "how" [of this transformation]. The external appearance of the transformed one will remain virtually unchanged. However, a terrible and frightening energy will proceed from him.... Anyone who touches him will receive an electric shock. An invincible hypnotic force [will proceed from him].... The disturbing influence...[upon spiritually striving human beings] and upon the entire population that will be set in motion by the transformation of the Antilogos will be extraordinary.... After a rigged vote, he—the miracle worker—will crown himself.... Humanity will be divided [into those who accept him as world ruler]...and those who refuse to acknowledge the usurper....

Of course, force will be used against anyone who refuses to follow the Antichrist. Dark miracles will occur increasingly, shattering the consciousness of human beings to the very roots of their being. For many, Christ's miracles will pale into insignificance. Crazy enthusiasm will roll in waves across the world.... Eventually the Antilogos will hold the sole rulership of the planet in his hands. Yet the true, highest leaders will not subject themselves to the usurper. And this will also be the case for millions or perhaps hundreds of millions of people in all countries of the world.

The age of persecution commences. From year to year they become more and more extensive, methodical, [and] cruel. Here the cunning Gagtungr [Ahriman/Satan] even makes use of the heroic protest of the masses. The candidate for the Antichrist who had failed...who had taken his life at the end of World War II,[4] advances now to become the self-appointed leader of the rebels in the struggle against the world ruler.... His thoroughly dark movement will draw the hearts of many into a spiral of raging wickedness and senseless hatred.... Christ's significance will continually be weakened. Then his name will be denied—and finally enveloped in silence....

Shock and terror will take hold of many. Millions of those who had previously distanced themselves from religious questions, who were primarily occupied with their concerns in their own little world or with artistic pursuits or scientific research, will sense that they are confronted with an irrevocable and very dangerous choice, in the face of which even torture and execution pale.... Countless people will turn away from this offspring of hell...from the dark miracles and the charm of the superman as well as from his immeasurable intelligence and frighteningly cynical wickedness.... The majority of people will fall away from God and allow themselves to be led astray by Gagtungr's protégée....

---

4   Daniel Andreev depicts the two main candidates for the Antichrist in their twentieth century incarnations as Adolf Hitler and Joseph Stalin. In these incarnations in the twentieth century, they were competing with each other as to who could be the most evil—in order then, in the following incarnation, to be the vessel for the incarnation of the Antichrist. According to Daniel Andreev, Joseph Stalin outdid Adolf Hitler in this contest to become the chosen one of the prince of darkness (footnote by RP).

Stalin wanted not only to be feared; he wanted also to be loved. The Antichrist, however, has need of only one thing: the conviction that [should be held by] everyone without exception, [to] believe in his superiority and [to] subject themselves to him without any hesitation....

When [during the reign of the Antichrist] the machine civilization begins its total assault on Nature, the entire landscape of the Earth's surface will be transformed into a complete Anti-Nature.... Nature, having become inwardly empty and outwardly crippled, will no longer awaken aesthetic or pantheistic feelings....

Certainly, also during the total rulership of the tyrant, there will be not a few human beings whose innermost life will rebel against the senseless existence under the Antichrist. However, psychic control will already stifle such thoughts as soon as they arise, and only a few will succeed in acquiring a system of psychic self-defense that will protect them from being physically destroyed....

All written or other testimonies that could be dangerous for the Antichrist will be destroyed....

[The suffering of human beings gives nourishment (*gavvach*) to the demons.]... No world wars, revolutions, repressions, no mass spilling of blood, could have produced *gavvach* in such amounts.... Actually, even humanity in its demonized aspect will not satisfy the Antichrist. He needs humanity as his source of *gavvach*.... [However] even in the most sinful soul, there gleams an inextinguishable spark of conscience. But also despair, dumbing down, and sheer boredom with life will take hold of many people, and this will lead to their rejection by the Antichrist. What use to him is the intellectual paralysis that sets in after such excesses of despair? These people are hardly suited to the further development of demonic science and technology or the conquest of the cosmos or the satanization of the world....

[After the death of the Antichrist] the world state rapidly collapses and it is only through drastic measures that anarchy in various parts of the world is hindered.... "And there appears a great sign in heaven: a woman clothed with the Sun" [Revelation 12:1].... Who is the *woman clothed with the Sun*? It is Sventa-Sventana [Sophia], embraced by the planetary Logos and chosen to give birth to the

Great Spirit of the Second Aeon. The mirroring of this event in world history is the Rose of the World, whose utmost striving before, during, and after the time of the Antichrist prepares humanity to become a vessel for the Great Spirit.... An unimaginable jubilation takes hold of this and other worlds, and humanity passes through a great, light-filled transformation.

The prince of darkness will terrify human beings.... Christ, however, will take on as many forms as there are consciousnesses on Earth to behold him. He will adapt himself to everyone, and will converse with all. His forms, in an unimaginable way, will simultaneously yield an image: *One who appears in heaven surrounded by unspeakable glory.* There will not be a single being on Earth who will not see the Son of God and hear his Word.

✝

These words by Daniel Andreev are prophetic in nature. They were written shortly before his death in 1959, and now, more than fifty years later, not only is the encounter with the Son of God possible, but also the hearing of his Word. At the present time, it is this meeting with the Son of God in the realm where he can now be experienced, the realm of life forces known as the *etheric realm*, which is the most important event that anyone in earthly existence can experience. This is the spiritual event that is the initiatory aspect of the encounter with the Antichrist as the initiation trial for humanity as a whole crossing the threshold.

As an example of this spiritual event, included here is the account of a young woman, Estelle Isaacson, of her initiatory experience in meeting Christ as the Greater Guardian of the threshold. This description of her meeting with Christ in the etheric realm—with the Etheric Christ (to use Rudolf Steiner's expression)—can be a source of inspiration to everyone. In a vision she had on September 11, 2009, she describes that she came to this experience of the Etheric Christ through meditating upon Christ's experiences during the night prior to the Mystery of Golgotha, the night in the Garden of Gethsemane:

✝

When a human being enters into the event of Gethsemane and beholds His suffering, the light of His deed is released again into the heavens, which causes the spiritual beings to take notice of the Earth, and come to her aid—but also attracts the dark side as well. The light of Christ prevails over the darkness; it prevails for human beings who are willing to gaze upon the deeds of Christ (His Passion) and accept His sacrifice. Any human being who will meditate upon the event of Gethsemane, and who can truly speak the words, *"Not my will, but Thine,"* radiates great light out into the cosmos; angels come running to join with the light. And within the heart of each angel is a reflector, which reflects the light out into the heavens. The angels rejoice in the opportunity to be able to send this light out! They reflect the light back to the Earth as a gift; and when this happens, humans are awakened to the True Light. They start to feel the presence of Christ. They hear His Words; they see His Light. When they are awakened to the Light, they reflect it to other human beings—and not only this, but they reflect it to Nature. The Light of Christ awakens and vivifies Nature through the reflection of it by human beings.

The Etheric Christ said to me, *"Place your hands on My body* (the body of Jesus) *and allow the light to be taken in through the wounds of your hands. Let this light penetrate to your heart."* I placed my hands on the shoulders of Christ Jesus, who was bleeding from every pore—bleeding light out into the cosmos. I felt the light rise up in me and fill my entire being, penetrating my heart. It was completely indescribable!

"You Are the Light of the World"

I then merged with the Earth to an unfathomable degree—never before had I experienced such a merging. I became the "eye of the Earth"—it was as if I was the Earth, and the Earth had become an eye. I experienced myself as being at the center of the eye, which was also the Heart of Christ; as I looked out, I beheld the heavens—from the perspective of Earth beholding the heavens! I felt that the "eye" of the Earth cannot always behold the heavens; it is as if it remains asleep, until these moments when the Light awakens the Earth—then it is able to behold the heavens, and also be *known*. Again, I am trying to find an earthly way to describe something for which there is a lack of words! Seeing through the eye of Earth, gazing out into the heavens, I saw angels coming to grace the Earth with their presence. One of the angels came forward and placed a crystal inside of my heart—it had many facets and was a specific geometric formation. Upon placing it inside of my heart, the angel said, *"You are the light of the world!"* The angels were in a state of gratitude to me for being willing to accept the light—which could only come through great suffering. Christ spoke the same words to His disciples when He said, *"You are the light of the world."* And He said that they were a "city on a hill;" I saw how the light of the "city on the hill" shines out into the heavens and vanquishes the Foe! Christ also said to me, *"Your tears are the salt of the Earth. Your blood is the light, for even as light is taken in by your heart, it then enters into the blood, and thus you become a living light. And the light shall not be quenched, for the angels protect and guard the heart that bears the Light of Christ."*

My focus was again turned to Gethsemane; I entered into the light of His deed in the garden with my whole being and went into a state of ecstasy—an ineffable, unutterable ecstasy. The light of Christ in Gethsemane enveloped the Earth—up to that point, I had never merged with such light before. My heart soared in ecstasy, lifted up into another realm of spirit! I exclaimed, *"This is Life! This is Life eternal, the Life of the world. This is Love! This is eternal Love that knows no boundaries, for it has penetrated everything in the Earth. It lives within the Earth as an eternal promise of redemption. His love is eternal; His love is free for all who will accept it!"*

Christ then gave me a message for all: *"Love one another and love the Earth. Send your love to your fellow beings and into the Earth that the Earth may be lifted up on wings of peace. There is a body of the Earth, which is a body of love; this is My body that I gave to the Earth. You become one with the body of love by doing works of love, by cultivating feelings of love and by thinking thoughts of love. I invite all to become one with Me in this body of love. I call you home; My arms are around you. Return to love. Remember love. For where love is there am I; and because I desire to have you in My heart, I ask you to love one another, that I may be in you and you in Me. Look for Me to come to you for I am coming and shall gather you to myself and you shall be safely folded in Me because you are precious in My sight; and My sight is ever upon you. Return to Me...."* I then gazed upon Him, embracing all of the cosmos, His arms outstretched across the expanse of Heaven, and His voice penetrating the depths of my heart with these words: *"I AM eternally here!"*

As with the vision of Estelle Isaacson on pages 75 to 80, this vision is best read aloud and - better still - in a group, in the spirit of Christ's words: "Where two or three are gathered in my name, there am I in your midst" (Matthew 18:20). These visions, as some have experienced, have the power of invoking the *Parousia,* the Presence of Christ.

APPENDIX II
THE MYSTERY OF EVIL—OCCULT POSSESSION

BY DANIEL ANDREEV

In this excerpt, Daniel Andreev first discusses the role of *Hochha*[1] in the personality of the "grand inquisitor," whom he identifies as the preceding incarnation of Stalin, and then in the life of Stalin himself. It is important to bear in mind that this section of the Russian original of Rosa Mira was written in 1958 and that Stalin died in 1953.[2]

The last time that he entered the historical arena, it was in the figure whom Dostoevsky presented with meta-historical acumen as the "grand inquisitor." He was no Torquemada. He belonged neither to the highest nor to the lowest ranks of that Satanic experiment [the Spanish Inquisition]. He appeared as the political wave [of the Spanish Inquisition] was already fading away. In the course of his long life it became clear to him that the goal toward world tyranny could not be attained by way of transforming the Catholic Church into a mechanism functioning according to Gagtungr's will [Gagtungr is the Prince of Darkness, known as Ahriman in the Persian tradition and as Satan in the Judeo-Christian tradition].[3] However, his activity in the realm of the [Spanish] Inquisition gave him much, forcibly stimulating

---

1   The "ch" in *Hochha* is pronounced like the "ch" in *Loch* Ness Monster or like the "ch" in the name of the German composer *Bach*. It is not the same as "ck" or "k"; it is much more like a guttural, aspirated "h" sound.

2   Excerpted from the German translation of Daniel Andreev's magnum opus, *Rosa Mira, The Rose of the World*, written in Russian between December 24, 1950, and October 12, 1958, and first published as a book in Moscow in 1991. The translation of this excerpt by Robert Powell is from the German translation of *Rosa Mira*, volume 3, pages 55 to 57 and 88 to 118. Footnotes and remarks in brackets [ ] are by the translator.

3   From the glossary to the English edition of the *Rose of the World*: "*Gagtungr*=the name of the planetary demon.... He is three persons in one.... The first hypostasis of *Gagtungr* is *Gisturg*, the Great Torturer; the

him along the path of the will-to-power, bloodthirstiness, and sadistic cruelty—and thus created a channel for the working into his awake day consciousness of Gagtungr or, to be more precise, Urparp. From time to time, he was inspired not only through memories [from earlier incarnations] in the depth of his being, but also directly through his waking intelligence.

There is a special term—*Hochha*—which means "Satanic enlightenment." It is a matter of an ecstatic condition in which a human being communes with lofty demonic powers—not in trance, not in sleep, but in full possession of consciousness. Hochha became accessible to this being in Spain in the sixteenth century, thus attaining the level of conscious Satanism.

The time between this incarnation and the following one [as Stalin] at first naturally took its course in the region into which... the astral body was cast on account of the burden of a horrific destiny. Then this potential Antichrist was brought into Gashsharva,[4] where for more than two hundred years he was prepared for a new incarnation....

In a small land [Georgia] at the border between Asia and Europe, in a tiny mountain village, into a poor family of believers [Christians], this being saw again the light of day [on December 6, 1878, in the Russian Old Style calendar; he not only later changed his name from Ioseb Besarionis dze Jughashvili to Joseph Stalin, but also deliberately concealed his true birth date of December 6, 1878, later officially declaring that he had been born on December 21, 1879].... Urparp knew better than all others that this [incarnation] was not to be the main performance, but rather a rehearsal [for his potential role of the Antichrist in the next incarnation after that of Stalin]....

Even the childhood portrait of this being, when one looks at it more closely, is alarming.... A long and narrow chin, which became broader with increasing age. A prominent aggressive nose. In the facial contour of the pale, dry, pursed lips is mirrored stubbornness, lack of

---

second is *Fokerma*, the Great Harlot; and the third is *Urparp*, the great implementer of the demonic plan."

4   From the glossary in the English translation of the *Rose of the World*: "*Gashsharva*—one of the principal planes in the demonic anticosmos... where a variety of powerful demonic beings abide."

Joseph Stalin in his youth

heart, and a peculiar intellectual dullness. And now the eyes: strenuously focussed, they gaze sullenly, self-consciously, and hostilely at everything they set their gaze upon—no child should be exposed to this image (above).

For thirty years, the portrait of this being was impressed upon us—of course, not this youthful image, but the adult portrait. One could not take a step to the right or left, in front or behind, without encountering an image of his face. And it is not easy to free oneself from all connection with this image of his face, to rid oneself of the multitude of associations that it calls forth.... He created a cultural climate in which even the cleverest mind had de facto no possibility of raising his or her voice against the regime. He built up a security apparatus that protected the life of the ruler, making him unassailable to any kind of attack, whether from poison, dagger, bullet, or bomb. He put several million innocent people behind bars and united the voices of the remaining population into a never-ending hymn: to him, only to him, the beloved, the wise, the trusted ruler....

Massive repression began.[5] [The campaign directed against so-called terrorists] was senseless and completely indiscriminate. Accusations were made up, often "proved" by use of torture of the most cruel kind, taking place in "special camps" that make Auschwitz and Buchenwald pale into insignificance.... With this [extraordinary suffering], Stalin revealed himself not as an instrument of the third Witzraor [Shrugr], but as an instrument of the Great Torturer himself, since only Gagtungr and the demons of Gashsharva craved for Gavvakh in such unbelievable amounts.[6]

It seems that it has already been forgotten how this particular personality imprinted the stamp of his being upon a whole society through his exclusively private and personal inclinations. Stalin liked to work at night.... [Around the time of his seventieth birthday, 1948/1949] he was at the height of his power. Soon his last great international action would culminate in the establishment of communism in China. Yet what made him so melancholy?... It was the knowledge concerning what was taking place beyond the Earth, knowledge that he attained in the condition of Hochha.

It is not known to me whether anyone ever saw him in this condition. In the 1930s and 1940s, he had mastered the attainment of Hochha so well that he could to a certain extent call it forth at wish. Usually, it took place toward the end of the night, more often in winter than in summer, when the early sunrise disturbed it. Everyone thought that he would be resting, sleeping, and of course under no circumstances would anyone have dared to disturb his rest. In any case, no one would have been able to enter, even if they had wanted to, since he locked the door from the inside.

The light in the room was dimmed, but not completely out. If someone had come into the room invisibly at this hour, they would not have found the Führer [Vozhd] sleeping, but rather reclining in his great armchair. His face was completely changed, and it was a

---

5   During the 1930s, Stalin launched a campaign accusing people of terrorism. This grand purge was completely indiscriminate. Targets were executed, imprisoned in Gulag labor camps, or exiled.

6   From the glossary to the English edition of the *Rose of the World*: "*Gavvakh*—Radiations from human suffering...replenishes the energy of many categories of demonic beings and of *Gagtungr* himself."

shocking sight. The black eyes were wide-open in a fixed gaze staring into space. There was a peculiar reddish blush on his cheeks, which lost their usual pallid color. The wrinkles were smoothed out so that the whole face appeared much younger. The skin on the forehead was so smoothed out that the forehead appeared higher. The breaths were very deep and were few and far between. The arms were resting on the supporting arms of the armchair and the fingers occasionally tapped lightly on the sides.

To be precise, Hochha is not a definite condition, but rather a cycle of various conditions, varying according to which dark hierarchy the seer enters into connection with at that moment. At any rate, he perceives the physical objects in his surroundings only indistinctly against the background of the images from other levels of existence. If through some kind of miracle somebody would have entered the room, the enraptured one would have been able to recognize them and would have—even if not immediately—been able to return to the normal level [of consciousness]. During the condition of Hochha, Stalin turned most frequently to the grand Igva of Drukkarg and to Shrugr.[7] Sometimes he also had the honor of being inspired through Urparp himself.[8] Moreover, he was accompanied by yet another invisible being as his constant counsellor—an inhabitant of Gashsharva

---

7   From the glossary to the English edition of the *Rose of the World*: "*Igvas*— the principle race of antihumankind; it is made up of highly intelligent demonic beings who abide in the *Shrastrs*, the "underside of the world."

   "*Shrastrs*—variodimensional material worlds connected with areas within the physical body of the Earth known as *counterprevailing prominences*, which point to the center of the planet. The abode of antihumankind, which is composed of two races—*Igvas* and *Raruggs*. There are great metropolises in the *Shrastrs* and a very advanced demonic technology.

   "*Drukkarg*—the *Shrastr* of the Russian metaculture.

   "*Shrugr* is the Russian *Witzraor*.

   "*Witzraors*—powerful, intelligent, and extremely predatory beings that abide on planes adjacent to the *Shrastrs*. From the human point of view, the *Witzraors* are demons of state power. There are very few of them. *Witzraors* play a colossal, conflicting, and double-edged role in metahistory."

8   From page 54 of volume 3 of the German edition of *Rosa Mira* (*Rose of the World*): "Behind the figures of the two *Führer* [Lenin and Stalin] of revolutionary Russia, one saw not only the outline of the third Russian *Witzraor* [*Shrugr*] but also the clear shadow of an incomparably more powerful being—the one who on a planetary scale brings to realization the great demonic plan and who bears the name *Urparp*."

specially assigned to him.... In Hochha, Stalin went down into Gashsharva a number of times, into Drukkarg, where he saw not only the grand Igva but also a number of other beings. Hochha poured a massive quantity of energy into his being, and in the morning, when he appeared in his circle of his close comrades, he surprised them by his superhuman radiation of energy. This of itself sufficed for them to subjugate their will to him....

The demonic powers constantly wove around Stalin an impenetrable cocoon of darkness. In this way, he remained inaccessible to the powers of providence. Only once—and that only for a short moment—the cocoon was torn open. As Stalin was not in Hochha at that moment...the future stages of his own path were shown to him: his possible [next] incarnation as the Antichrist, and in the wake of that the subsequent catastrophic plunge down into the pit of the galaxy, where all time ceases—into a world of suffering such as, in terms of its hopelessness and relentless intensity, exists nowhere else in the universe. This was a night of unspeakable dread, so that through his whole being for some minutes a desperate prayer pervaded him, that he might be saved and prevented from proceeding further on the chosen path. Minutes went by. Pride, unbending rigidity, and the infinite striving for power gained the upper hand anew. However, that night in 1952 worked on for him. From that time on, when he put himself in Hochha, he no longer experienced the usual influx of energy. Perhaps, too, the effect of the strong psychological tension took its toll, the tension of continually having to wear the mask of materialistic Marxism, constantly having to lead a double life. Somehow he had overdone it, and only Shrugr still allowed forces to reach him through his constant channel of inspiration. Within a short time, the Führer [*Vozhd*] aged, and through the burden of continual physical illness, the balance of his psyche broke permanently....

In the early days of 1953...the channel of inspiration connecting the being of the [Russian] Witzraor [Shrugr] with his human instrument was broken off all of a sudden.... This took place at approximately 2 AM. Within half an hour, his consciousness was extinguished. However, the agony continued, as is known, for a few more days.

Urparp seized the broken channel and tried to breathe strength and consciousness back into the dying one. This was unsuccessful, thanks to some people who, in the midst of the tumult surrounding his death bed, endeavoured not to allow Stalin to return to life again....

At last came the great moment. Stalin breathed his last breath. Gashsharva quaked at this blow. In Drukkarg, the cries of terror and hate resounded. Shrugr howled on account of his pain and anger. Armies of demons arose from the depths into the upper layers of the subterranean realms and attempted to halt the plunge of the deceased one into the abyss of magma....

Only as the instrument of a Witzraor, far-removed from all humanness, would he return to wage a war leaving behind a lunar landscape in the place of Europe, Asia, and America, with the aim of physically surviving in the deepest hole on the Earth, and to arise from this hole as ruler over the remainder of humanity.... There remains only one guaranty as the indestructible foundation of all hope and consolation. If the world could succeed in averting the great war [World War III], then Rosa Mira, the Rose of the World, will arise, inevitably and irrevocably, at first in some democratic country, and then in another, continuing until She illumines all regions of the Earth...uniting people of higher spirituality from all parts of the world into a spiritual union.

Appendix III
2012 and World Pentecost

This appendix focuses upon this special time leading up to the pivotal year 2012, the deeper significance of which is discussed here in the context of Rudolf Steiner's prophecy of the World Pentecost. The content of this appendix is an edited version of the transcript of my lecture on World Pentecost, held July 24, 2009, in Chapel Hill, North Carolina.[1] This appendix addresses, from a different standpoint, a part of the book written by Kevin Dann and me, *Christ & the Maya Calendar*.[2] A central theme of the book is the year 2012. This point in time is the end date of the Maya Long Count Calendar, which is coming to an end at the winter solstice of the year 2012, specifically December 21, 2012. Many books have been written about this date. Some authors are prophesying a variety of catastrophes, while others are saying that we are going to wake up on December 22, 2012, and find ourselves in a kind of paradise, with all the terrible things occurring here on the Earth finished ("over and done with"). These are two extremes, and obviously it is not so simple.

The Maya Long Count Calendar began a long time ago, in the year 3114 BC, specifically August 11, 3114 BC (Gregorian calendar date). Historians use a method of dating that excludes the year zero, referring to 3114 BC. Astronomers have a slightly different method of dating. For astronomers, 3114 BC is the year -3113. Because historians go straight from 1 BC to AD 1, excluding the year zero, astronomers

---

1   In gratitude to Kelly Calegar, who organized the lecture and two subsequent workshops in Chapel Hill, and who transcribed the lecture.

2   Powell & Dann, *Christ & the Maya Calendar.*

identify 1 BC as the year zero, 2 BC as the year -1, 3 BC as the year -2, and so on, and this makes it a lot easier for computation with dates, by including the year zero. Given that the Maya Long Count calendar began in -3113 and finishes in 2012, we can add 2012 and -3113 and deduce that this calendar lasts for a total of 5,125 years.

The classical Maya culture flourished from between about AD 250 to around 900, a period of almost 700 years. During that time, the Maya civilization flourished as an agriculturally intensive and city-centered culture. It was a period of large-scale construction and the recording of inscriptions on monuments, exemplifying a significant intellectual and artistic development, the most notable monuments being their stepped pyramids. There were a number of remarkable Maya cities in Mesoamerica, and it was a culture that included highly developed art and architecture, agriculture and astronomy. Then this culture collapsed in a relatively short period of time, whereby most of the cities were abandoned, although some Maya cities in the Yucatan continued to flourish for centuries more until the Yucatan was conquered by the Spanish in the sixteenth century. Although many ideas have been put forward to explain the collapse of the classical Maya civilization, to this day we do not know with any degree of certainty what really happened. All kinds of monuments were left behind. During the twentieth century, these were decoded and the few surviving Maya texts were deciphered. From this breakthrough came the discovery that there were actually three calendars that the Maya used. The one that ends in the year 2012 is called the Maya Long Count Calendar. What is this calendar about?

Although the Maya retreated from their cities, there are at the present time still about seven million descendants of the Maya in southern Mexico, the Yucatan Peninsula, Guatemala, Belize, El Salvador, and western Honduras. From those who have done research among these descendants, there is some knowledge of the ideas and beliefs of the Maya. For example, it is surmised that the period of 5,125 years of the Long Count Calendar is what the Maya called the fourth age, or Age of the Fourth Sun. The fourth age is followed by the fifth age, and anyone who has studied chronology can recognize that here there is a parallel with Hindu chronology,[3] in which the ages are called "Yugas." According to the book called The Laws of Manu, we are still in the fourth age, or fourth Yuga, referred to as the Kali Yuga. Hindu chronology refers to a sequence of four Yugas, whose names are Krita Yuga, Treta Yuga, Dvapara Yuga, and Kali Yuga. Then, according to some Hindu sources, will follow the fifth Yuga, called Satya Yuga. *Yuga* means simply "age."

This teaching of the Yugas became transmitted to Greece, where expressions were used that are more familiar to us. The Greek poet Hesiod, for instance, used the designations Golden Age, Silver Age, Bronze Age, and Iron Age. The Iron Age of the Greeks corresponds to the Hindu Dark Age or Kali Yuga. Against the background of Hindu chronology, we have a fairly clear idea of what is signified by the succession of ages or Yugas.

It is striking that in Hindu chronology the fourth age, Kali Yuga, began very close in time to the start of the fourth age in the Maya calendar. Kali Yuga, according to Hindu chronology, began at midnight on February 17/18, 3102 BC (astronomers would say, in the year -3101). This date differs by merely twelve years from the start of the Maya Long Count Calendar. Clearly, there is a correspondence here. However, according to the dating for the Kali Yuga originally derived from the ancient Sanskrit text entitled The Laws of Manu, it is stated that the Kali Yuga lasts for 432,000 years. If we accept this dating, it would imply that at the present time we are less than 5,120 years into Kali Yuga, which then would last a further (approximately) 427,000 years.

Interestingly, there are Hindu teachers, including Sri Yukteswar, the teacher of Yogananda,[4] who indicated that one has to look at the dating of the Yugas differently—that they are not the purported great, lengthy periods of time. Another individual who also took up the theme of the dating of the Yugas was Rudolf Steiner, who mentioned on various occasions that Kali Yuga lasted for a period of five

---

3   Ibid., chapter 6, for the parallel between the Hindu Yugas and the Maya calendar.

4   Yogananda came from India to the United States and founded the Self Realization fellowship in Southern California in 1920.

thousand years. My astrosophical research confirms this indication, and I was able to determine the end date of Kali Yuga to be September 10, 1899.[5] Between -3101 and 1899, five thousand years elapsed, this being the length of Kali Yuga, which is regarded as the fourth age.

Moreover, Rudolf Steiner gave a very precise meaning to the ending of the fourth age, Kali Yuga. He spoke of the New Age, the Age of Light, which then began in 1899. In Hindu chronology, according to some sources, the Age of Light is Satya Yuga, the fifth age that follows the fourth age, Kali Yuga. This fifth age or Satya Yuga, according to Rudolf Steiner, has to do with an event he refers to as the Second Coming of Christ, which, however, is not the return of Christ in a physical body. Instead, Christ's return is in an ethereal body, a body of light. Through his reappearance in the world of the etheric, the invisible world of life forces, Christ has the ability to appear simultaneously to people in different places around the world. This is occurring now, during this Age of Light (Satya Yuga) that began in 1899.[6]

Following these indications, I have written a book about this called *The Christ Mystery,* in which I translated into English various accounts of people who have had experiences of Christ in his ethereal form.[7] The experiences described there generally occurred as a matter of grace, and on the whole they are very beautiful and profound life-changing experiences. In November 2008, I had the good fortune of meeting a young woman, Judith von Halle, who on Good Friday in 2004 received the stigmata, which are the visible wounds/signs of Christ.[8] She is Jewish, and it is very unusual for a Jewish woman to

---

5   Powell, *Chronicle of the Living Christ,* p. 418. See also, Powell, *The Christ Mystery: Reflections on the Second Coming.*

6   Steiner, *The Reappearance of Christ in the Etheric,* lecture of January 25, 1910.

7   Powell, *The Christ Mystery,* chapter 1.

8   Judith von Halle was born in Berlin in 1972. She attended school in Germany and the U.S. and studied architecture, graduating in 1998. She encountered Anthroposophy in 1997 and began working as a staff member at Rudolf Steiner House in Berlin, where she also lectured from 2001, while maintaining an architectural practice. In 2004, her life was transformed when she received the stigmata. Her first book was published in German in 2005, and she now works principally as a lecturer and author. She lives part of the time in Berlin and for the remaining time in Dornach, Switzerland. Among her books in

receive this grace of bearing the stigmata—perhaps it is even the first such case. In addition, she is not Catholic; until now, virtually all recorded cases of the stigmata have been within the Catholic Church. Moreover, Judith von Halle is an Anthroposophist who has studied the works of Rudolf Steiner. What is striking about her experience is that, until she received the stigmata, she enjoyed eating; but from the time she received the stigmata, she found she was no longer able to eat any food. In fact, eating made her ill. Now her only intake is water, and this only occasionally.

When I met her in November 2008, she had not eaten for four and a half years, yet she was radiantly healthy! In terms of her consciousness, an incredible change came about when she received the stigmata. She came into communion with Christ. In particular, she came into communion with the resurrection body of Christ. Through this communion with the resurrection body of Christ, she receives all she needs to live.[9] She does not need anything else. She receives such abundance from the communion with Christ's resurrection body that she does not need any physical nourishment. She is a living testimony to Steiner's indication about the reappearance of Christ and that through this new and living relationship with Christ, human beings will have the possibility of undergoing a dramatic change of consciousness. Judith von Halle has indeed gone through a remarkable change of consciousness since receiving the stigmata at Easter 2004.

It was a significant meeting, to meet someone who is in contact with the living Christ to such a degree that she has received the visible wounds of Christ, the stigmata. She is a remarkable testimony to the unfolding of the New Age which, in light of Rudolf Steiner's indications, is the age of Christ's Second Coming. Today, the expression "New Age" is well known; it is a widely used expression. However,

---

English translation are the following: *And If He Had Not Been Raised...*: *The Stations of Christ's Path to Spirit Man* (2007); *The Lord's Prayer: The Living Word of God* (2007); *Illness and Healing: The Mystery Language of the Gospels* (2008); *Secrets of the Stations of the Cross and the Grail Blood: The Mystery of Transformation* (2008); and *Descent into the Depths of the Earth on the Anthroposophic Path of Schooling* (2011).

9   Von Halle, *And If He Had Not Been Raised...*, p. 23: "The life-force emanating from the Resurrection strengthens me inwardly so much that I can be outwardly nourished by it."

most people do not realize that it was Rudolf Steiner who introduced this term and that it has a very explicit meaning having to do with the return of Christ in an ethereal form—his Second Coming. To summarize: the end of Kali Yuga, the Dark Age, in 1899 heralded the beginning of the New Age, the Age of Light, Satya Yuga, the age of Christ's Second Coming. However, there is still the question what this has to do with the year 2012? In order to grasp this connection, we need to consider first the Hindu understanding of Kali Yuga.

The Hindu understanding of the starting date of Kali Yuga is that it was also the death date of Krishna. In India there are a tremendous number of gods and goddesses who are revered in the Hindu religion. There are many different spiritual groups and movements. But all love Krishna! Krishna is the central figure in Hinduism. Rudolf Steiner spoke about Krishna, and what he indicated points to a relationship between Krishna and Jesus. Rudolf Steiner, when speaking of Jesus of Nazareth, spoke of a pure soul that had never gone through the event of the Fall, a pure soul that had come into incarnation on the Earth for the first time as Jesus. In other words, Jesus of Nazareth had never been incarnated on the Earth before and was therefore a pure being. However, Steiner also indicated that even though Jesus had not been incarnated on the Earth before, he had worked from higher realms to assist humankind on the path of spiritual evolution. In fact, according to Steiner, Jesus of Nazareth is the same being who in the Hindu religion is called Krishna—in other words, Krishna and Jesus are one and the same.[10]

If we read the Bhagavad Gita carefully as the primary source for our understanding of Krishna and the most widely known Hindu sacred scripture, we come to recognize that Krishna had not been incarnated in a physical body but had "overlighted" an individual and taught through that individual. Krishna was not actually incarnated but was overlighting Arjuna the charioteer. The teachings of Krishna were presented through Arjuna. When speaking of the "death" of Krishna at that point in time, at the start of Kali Yuga, what is really meant by this is that the "death" of Krishna was actually the event of Krishna withdrawing from Arjuna to return to higher realms. The

---

10   Steiner, *The Bhagavad Gita and the West.*

remarkable level of consciousness that Arjuna had attained through being overlighted by Krishna was no longer. For Arjuna it meant darkness; he had been enveloped in the incredible light coming from Krishna, and then, when Krishna "died"—or rather, withdrew—Arjuna experienced darkness.

This experience was symptomatic for nearly all human beings who would experience this darkness sooner or later in the subsequent period of time, during the course of Kali Yuga. It was indicative of the future period of time in which humanity would experience the loss of light consciousness, which is why this time period is called the Dark Age, or Kali Yuga. In our time we find this darkness to be the normal state of consciousness. Generally we are not aware of our spiritual origin—that we are divine beings who have incarnated here upon the Earth. In addition, we are usually unaware of our previous lives on the Earth, let alone our experience in spiritual realms in between incarnations on this planet. Thus, more often than not, we are unaware of who we are in a deeper sense or where we were before we came into existence here on Earth. From the standpoint of Krishna consciousness, which Arjuna received through being overlighted, we are living in darkness. Now, the Age of Light means the coming again of this same being who overlighted Arjuna and was then incarnated as Jesus of Nazareth. Through his Second Coming he is again awakening the light-filled consciousness that existed at the time of Krishna/Arjuna and which, later, various people received through Christ—St. John, the author of the Book of Revelation, being a notable example of an individual who was overlighted by Jesus Christ.

We can find many outstanding examples of human beings who have attained this light consciousness even during the Dark Age. St. Paul, for example, had an experience of blinding light at the gates of Damascus through which he received an imprint of Christ Jesus, whom he then proclaimed on his travels to the different communities scattered around the Mediterranean. Other individuals, as well, attained this light-filled Christ consciousness that filled both Paul and John. These individuals were forerunners of the new experience of Christ that is opening up in our time. Through grace, they received

Christ consciousness even during the Dark Age of Kali Yuga. Now, during the New Age, Satya Yuga, we are coming into a time when more and more human beings are attaining Christ consciousness that existed in a preliminary form as Krishna consciousness in ancient times and which is reappearing in our time in a new way through the encounter with Christ in his Second Coming.

Judith von Halle, who I mentioned previously, is an example of someone who has come into this light-filled consciousness, from which she is able to communicate extraordinary things. Rudolf Steiner himself bore witness to the presence of Christ. He had a "Paul" or "Arjuna" experience in 1899, which he describes in his autobiography. Out of this direct experience he then began his life's work as a spiritual teacher to proclaim the reality of the event of Christ's return in a new form, an ethereal form, in our time. What Steiner stressed, however, is that we come into Christ consciousness, this light-filled conscious-ness of spiritual awareness, if we actively seek it, because Christ leaves us completely free, and if we do not ask, we do not receive, unless by virtue of grace. Generally speaking—although there are, as described earlier, also Christ encounters through grace—we come into Christ consciousness above all through actively seeking Christ. This is a very important consideration. The question is: What does all this have to do with the year 2012?

In *Christ & the Maya Calendar,* I indicated that we are able to come to a true understanding of the significance of the transition in 1899 from the Dark Age to the New Age of Light if we comprehend that since 1899 Christ is working in Earth's evolution in a new way. Yet, at the same time the impulses of the Dark Age continue on into the present time. In other words, since 1899 we are living in a period of a great epic struggle between the forces of light, led by Christ, and forces of darkness, which are opposing the light of Christ. In the Christian tradition the Letters of John refer to the Antichrist as the force opposing Christ. From the subtitle of *Christ & the Maya Calendar—2012 and the Coming of the Antichrist—*it is evident that this theme is a central focus in the book, the theme of the apocalyptic struggle between the forces of light and the forces of darkness since 1899 and continuing into our time.

Let us now consider the difference between the end date of the Kali Yuga according to Rudolf Steiner, which is the year 1899, and the end date of the Maya calendar, which is the year 2012. What is this difference about? My understanding is that the Maya astronomers were aware, like the Hindu chronologists, that humanity entered into a dark age that would end around the present time. As discussed above, looking at the starting points of both the Maya calendar (in 3114 BC) and Kali Yuga (in 3102 BC), there is only a twelve year difference between these two starting dates. However, what the Maya astronomers seemed to have grasped is that there would be a period of conflict between the forces of light and darkness before the real New Age would begin. That would explain why the Maya astronomers came to the year 2012 as the start of the New Age instead of the year 1899.

At this point in time we are rapidly approaching the year 2012. Summarizing the above: Rudolf Steiner spoke of 1899 as the start of the New Age, which can also be thought of as the Age of Christ's Second Coming. However, for those people who originally devised the Maya Calendar, it seems that they intuited that the real start of the New Age would not be until the year 2012, since they may have recognized the possibility that humanity must first pass through a little more than a century of experiencing the conflict between the forces of light and those of darkness—in the period from 1899 to 2012.

There is, moreover, a cosmological background to the 2012 date. In order to grasp this background, it requires that we first understand the structure of our galaxy. A map of the galaxy shows the center of the galaxy, called the Galactic Center (see image below). In the Platonic tradition that which was conceived to be at the Galactic Center was called the Supra-Celestial Sun, thought of as a Great Sun in the midst of the stars of our galaxy whereby, of course, the ancients had a completely different relationship to the heavens than we have now through modern astronomy, and so their understanding of the galaxy was quite different from ours.

As a point of departure, let us consider that all the stars in the heavens are Suns like our Sun. We can think of our Sun as our local star. Every single star, or Sun, is a miniature copy of the Supra-Celestial

Sun—at least, this was the conception in the Platonic stream to which Neoplatonists such as Proclus (412–485) belonged. I shall refer to it simply as the Central Sun, a term that conveniently expresses the fact that it is located at the center of the galaxy. The Central Sun is the Supra-Celestial Sun at the center of the galaxy, i.e. at the Galactic Center. However, it is to be noted that this is somewhat different from the understanding of modern astronomy. The current astronomical concept of the Galactic Center is that there is a super-massive black hole there, whereby it has to be borne in mind that this is purely a theoretical concept which is, moreover, an inadequate concept—one that does not grasp that in the central region of the galaxy, at the Galactic Center, there is the point of transition from creation to pure spirit, or vice versa from pure spirit to creation.

Everything has come into existence from the Central Sun. All the stars in our galaxy have been born, directly or indirectly, from this great center, which, if we were able to enter into this realm, we would find is a realm of pure spirit.[11] In the book *Christ & the Maya Calendar*, there is an appendix about the Central Sun, revealing that it is not at all a super-massive black hole. It is a great center that can be thought of as the Divine Heart of our galaxy, supporting everything in the galaxy, just as the heart maintains everything in the human organism. Ultimately it is the power of Divine Love that streams from this Divine Heart, the Central Sun. In the words of Dante it is a matter of, "The love that moves the Sun and the other stars" (*The Divine Comedy: Paradise* 33: 144–145). All the stars (our Sun is one of about 100 billion stars in the Milky Way galaxy) are orbiting around the Central Sun in a clockwise direction. Our Sun takes approximately 227 million years to go once around the Central Sun. On its passage around the Central Sun, it travels through different regions of the galaxy. This is a key concept for understanding what the Dark Age is and how it arose.

---

11   The expression "all the stars" has to be modified. Certainly it is true to say that all first generation stars have been born directly from the Galactic Center. However, there are second generation stars which have been born from first generation stars. For these second generation stars, therefore, it is appropriate to say that "by virtue of line of descent" they have been born from the Central Sun—in other words, indirectly (rather than directly).

Imagine walking in nature on a beautiful, sunny day and then an enormous black cloud comes and hides the Sun, so that the atmosphere grows cold and dark. In experiencing this, one knows that the Sun is going to re-appear and so normally one would not be overly concerned. By way of analogy, it may be surmised that it was something like this that Maya and Hindu chronologists perceived long ago in relation to the passage of our Sun around the Central Sun. Of course, they could not formulate it in this way, because at that time there was not a clear conception of the movement of our Sun around the Galactic Center. For us now, knowing of this movement by way of modern astronomy, the question is: What is emanating from the Central Sun that holds everything together (100 billion or more stars) in their orbits around this great center?

The answer lies in considering the Central Sun as the Ultimate Source of existence from which is streaming Divine Love, Light, and Life[12]—issuing forth from the Central Sun at the heart of our galaxy and sustaining all 100 billion stars in their orbits. This means that every star in the galaxy, including our Sun, receives from the Central Sun. In turn, from our Sun it is "stepped down" to a level of vibration appropriate for us here on the Earth. Thus, Divine Love—stepped down to an appropriate level—pours through our solar system, emanating from our Sun. Literally, our existence is maintained not only from the Sun but also in a larger sense from the Ultimate Source, the Central Sun.

The Sun moves in a clockwise direction around the Central Sun and the Earth moves in a counter clockwise direction around the Sun. Visualizing the yearly passage of the Earth around the Sun, there is a time each year when the Earth is between our Sun and the Central Sun. At this moment there is an alignment: Sun—Earth—Central Sun. Then, visualizing the Earth's passage continuing around the Sun, a new alignment occurs six months later in which, from the Earth, the Sun is seen in conjunction with the Central Sun. At this moment during the cycle of the year there is then a line, or alignment: Earth—Sun—Central Sun. At the present time in the twenty-first century, this

---

12 By way of abbreviation, "Divine Love, Light, and Life" is shortened in this appendix simply to "Divine Love."

The Milky Way Galaxy

alignment happens every year around December 18/19. Visualizing the Earth continuing to progress around the Sun, it returns again a further six months later to its position between the Sun and the Central Sun: Sun—Earth—Central Sun. This cosmic alignment happens six months later, because the Earth takes one year to go around the Sun, and between the two forms of alignment the Earth makes half a circuit around the Sun during which half a year elapses. At the present time, the cosmic alignment of the Earth between the Sun and the Central Sun happens every year around June 18/19 (six months after December 18/19). It was extraordinary to discover that this galactic alignment (Sun—Earth—Central Sun) took place at the historical event of Pentecost. When I discovered this, I realized that I had found an important key revealing that Christianity is a cosmic religion. The event of Pentecost was a cosmic event, a galactic alignment of the Earth with the Central Sun at the heart of our galaxy.

It is important to note that in our time the alignment of the Earth between the Central Sun and our Sun takes place June 18/19 each year. However, because of the phenomenon known as the precession of the equinoxes, this date changes in the course of the centuries. When we go back to the time of Christ, because of the shift that occurs on account of the precession of the equinoxes, this alignment was on a different date—on May 24, AD 33—which was the historical date of Pentecost. In *Chronicle of the Living Christ,* I have written how this date and many other dates in the life of Christ were determined with a very high degree of accuracy.

What took place at that historical event of Pentecost? If we take seriously the words of Christ, "I and the Father are one" (John 10:30), the implication is that Christ was one with the whole galaxy, that his being extended all the way up to the Galactic Center, the Divine Heart at the center of our galaxy. This consideration is supported by the statement made by Rudolf Steiner that every step that Christ took was in harmony with the whole universe:

> In Palestine during the time that Jesus of Nazareth walked on Earth as Jesus Christ—during the three years of His life, from His thirtieth to His thirty-third year—the entire being of the cosmic Christ was acting uninterruptedly upon Him, and was working into Him. The Christ stood always under the influence of the entire cosmos; He made no step without this working of the cosmic forces into and in Him.... It was always in accordance with the collective being of the whole universe with whom the Earth is in harmony, that all that Christ Jesus did took place.[13]

Thus, "I and the Father are one" could be formulated in modern language as "I and the collective being of the whole universe are one." At the time of Rudolf Steiner, during the first quarter of the twentieth century, "the universe" meant "the galaxy." There was no conception at that time, generally speaking, that there were other galaxies beyond our galaxy. Speaking of "the whole universe," Rudolf Steiner's words meant to his audience of that time "the whole Milky Way galaxy." In

---

13 Steiner, *Spiritual Guidance of the Individual and Humanity,* p. 28.

Illustration by Gustave Doré for Dante's Divine Comedy: Paradiso;
*Dante and Beatrice viewing the Empyrean in the form of a snow-white
rose (Empyrean derives from the Ancient Greek word "Pyr" meaning
fire, which reminds us of Daniel Andreev's expression
"Astrofire" for the Galactic Center)*

other words, Christ was connected with the whole Milky Way galaxy
with every step he took and, correspondingly, he was inwardly united
with the Central Sun, the Divine Heart at the center of our galaxy.

Let us now consider Dante's great vision from his extraordinary
poem *The Divine Comedy*. In the last half of *The Divine Comedy*, the
part entitled "Paradise," Dante describes being inwardly transported
to the highest realm of existence, which he refers to as the Empyrean.
In contemplating this image (above) which is a depiction by Gustav

Doré of Dante's experience of the Empyrean, is one not reminded of the image (page 111) depicting our galaxy?

This portrayal by Doré is of Dante's vision of the snow-white rose in the Empyrean. In the language of the Book of Revelation, what is here in the center of this celestial white rose is the Throne of God. Around the Throne of God are the angelic beings of the spiritual hierarchies, participating in the work of creation. The whole, in the words of Dante, is shaped in the form of a snow-white rose, which is also an image for Divine Sophia. In the mystical tradition—to which Daniel Andreev's *Rose of the World* is a recent contribution—Sophia is conceived of as being the celestial rose.[14] Sophia embodies the Wisdom ("plan") of creation. Sophia embraces the whole of our galaxy. Like Christ, she is an "offspring" of the Creator, a God-born being (rather than a created being like the angelic beings of the spiritual hierarchies). She embodies the plan of creation. Further, in the Book of Revelation, Sophia is referred to as the Bride of the Lamb. The Lamb is the expression used in the Book of Revelation for Christ. Sophia is the Divine Feminine counterpart of Christ. It thus emerges that Christ is a being who—like his Divine Feminine counterpart, Sophia—is connected with the whole Milky Way galaxy. Long ago Christ chose to incarnate upon the Earth in the human being Jesus of Nazareth—a process that extended over eons of time.[15]

From his vantage point in higher realms, the being we call Christ was able to see that humanity was entering a period of darkness, the dark age of Kali Yuga. He came in the middle of this Dark Age in order to bring the light of the Central Sun into the darkness. In the words from the prologue to the Gospel of St. John: "The light shines in the darkness, and the darkness overcometh it not" (John 1:5).

Christ incarnated to prepare a group of human beings, the twelve disciples, to be able to receive directly the Divine Love emanating from the Central Sun. Exactly this was the event of Pentecost. The work of Christ was to prepare this group of human beings to receive

---

14 Andreev, *The Rose of the World*; see also, Powell & Dann, *Christ & the Maya Calendar*, chapter 9 and appendix 1.

15 See Powell, "Sophia and the Rose of the World"; http://sophiafoundation.org/articles/.

the outpouring of Divine Love from the Central Sun. In the Christian tradition this is depicted as tongues of fire coming down on the heads of the disciples. Through this event the disciples became enlightened and transformed. Christ consciousness was born within them. They received the Holy Spirit, and they were then able to go out and teach and heal in the name of Christ. They became apostles.

The Holy Spirit is nothing other than the continual outpouring of Divine Love from the Central Sun—the pouring out of the fire of Divine Love that underlies all existence and which has brought all things into being. Christ came from the Central Sun and prepared a group of human beings on Earth to be able to receive at Pentecost the outpouring of Divine Love directly from the Central Sun, through which they came into Christ consciousness. Let us recall, as indicated above, that Pentecost on May 24, AD 33, was a cosmic event at which the alignment Sun—Earth—Central Sun took place.

According to Rudolf Steiner the event of Pentecost, which took place nearly two thousand years ago, is to become a world event. He spoke of this as the coming World Pentecost. What does he mean by this? The World Pentecost is an event comparable to Pentecost two thousand years ago. However, it will be a world event, not just an event that impacts a relatively small group of people in a particular geographical location. At that time in AD 33, it was a matter of several thousand people, initially the twelve disciples who became apostles went out onto the streets of Jerusalem, to the pool of Bethesda, and baptized three thousand people that day (and thousands more subsequently). In contrast, the World Pentecost will be an event of the outpouring of Divine Love for the whole of humanity. Will humanity be sufficiently prepared to receive this? And when is the World Pentecost going to happen? And, further, what might this foretell concerning our primary question regarding the significance of the year 2012?

Let us contemplate once again the movement of our Sun around the Central Sun. From the beginning of Kali Yuga or the Maya calendar, around 5,120 years ago, our Sun entered a part of the galaxy littered with debris from the Sagittarius Dwarf Galaxy. Our Sun thus came into a region of cosmic debris that acted as a shield of cosmic dust so that our Sun—and consequently the entire solar system—was no longer receiving the full outpouring of the great wave of Divine Love from the Central Sun. While the spiritual beings undergoing their evolution upon our Sun are at such a high level of spirituality that they are still able to focus upon and receive the outpouring of Divine Love from the Central Sun, this is not the case for most human beings on the Earth, with the exception of a few highly evolved spiritual masters. The Hindu and Maya astronomer-chronologists evidently intuited that this shielding effect impeding the inflow of the great wave of Divine Love from the Central Sun would last for only a limited period of time, as in the analogy used earlier of being out on a walk and experiencing the Sun disappearing behind a cloud, knowing that the Sun will eventually reappear from behind the cloud. The date of the start of the New Age has been a matter of forecasting when the Sun would pass out of the shielding effect of cosmic dust belonging to this part of the galaxy, where there are the remnants of the Sagittarius Dwarf Galaxy, a region through which our Sun has been passing for some 5,120 years. It is a matter of forecasting when our Sun will pass out from this galactic region of cosmic dust and debris to begin to receive again the great wave of Divine Love that is continually proceeding from the Central Sun. The prophecy of the Maya astronomers, who were attuned to the galactic level of existence, is that this will occur around the end of 2012. This is not so far away. According to the astrosophical research presented in this article, we are rapidly approaching the event of a galactic alignment at the winter solstice in 2012 through which humanity as a whole will receive a great wave of Divine Love—and this is precisely the event prophesied by Rudolf Steiner as the World Pentecost. Whether this event will occur exactly when the galactic alignment occurs on December 21, 2012, or whether it takes place at some later point in time (for example, around 2230—see below), it is important that we consciously prepare for it.

In using the expression galactic alignment in relation to the year 2012, it has to be clarified that this galactic alignment is not with the Central Sun as at the historical event of Pentecost. Rather, it has to do with the Sun at the winter solstice crossing the Galactic Equator during the 36-year period from 1980 to 2016, as discussed in *Christ & the Maya Calendar,* where the expression "2012 Window" is used to denote this 36-year period. It is important to point out that the galactic alignment of the winter solstice Sun with the Galactic Center will not take place until about the year 2230, which raises the question whether this will be the time of the World Pentecost rather than 2012? In the voluminous literature concerning the date of the end of the Maya calendar, 2012 is well known as falling within the period of 1980 to 2016 of the galactic alignment of the winter solstice Sun with the Galactic Equator. The new perspective offered in this appendix is that—if this date intuited by the Maya truly does denote the real start of the New Age—2012 marks the end of the (approximately) 5,120-year period of the Sun's passage through the local galactic region of cosmic dust and debris obscuring our solar system from the Central Sun and that the exit of our Sun from this dust-filled local galactic region signifies the (re-)opening to the great wave of Divine Love proceeding from the Central Sun and that this is the World Pentecost.

Obviously, it is important that as many people as possible know about this approaching event. For we can only receive the benefits of the great wave of Divine Love if we know about it and prepare for it; otherwise it is possible that we might experience it as a kind of scourging. How may this be understood?

There is a grand and magnificent painting by Michelangelo in the Sistine Chapel in Rome, The Last Judgment. There in the middle of this picture one sees Christ together with the Virgin Mary, surrounded by the apostles. One also sees on one side souls descending, fleeing away from Christ. These are referred to as the souls of the damned. On the other side one sees souls ascending; these souls, who are being drawn toward Christ, are called the souls of the blessed. This great work of art portrays the two possible ways of encountering the approaching great wave of Divine Love. In other words, the coming World Pentecost can be experienced either as a tremendous blessing or as a scourging. It will be experienced as a scourging if the presence of Divine Love calls forth shame for all of the negative things one has ever done, calling forth shame to such a degree that one is overwhelmed and one's inner response is to flee the World Conscience, who is Christ.

Potentially, therefore, shame can cause one to become overwhelmed to such a degree that it results in the impulse to flee. Therefore, in order to prepare for the World Pentecost, to be prepared to receive the powerful incoming wave of Divine Love, one needs to come to terms with one's shadow side, so that one is not overwhelmed by one's lower nature when it is exposed to the light of the World Conscience (Christ). A further important point in contemplating Michelangelo's great work of art is that Christ does not at all appear in a judgmental mode at the center of the painting. He appears in a blessing way. Nevertheless, judgment takes place simply by virtue of Christ's presence. The souls of the damned flee because their conscience shrinks in the face of the World Conscience (Christ), whereas the souls of the blessed, having attained a certain degree of expiation through raising the content of the subconscious into consciousness and thus purifying their lower nature, are attracted irresistibly toward the World Conscience.

Expressed in a positive way, we have to raise our level of vibration in order to come into and receive the approaching wave of Divine Love. Let us remember that this is an event that is happening on a global scale. Throughout the whole world human beings have to come to terms with the shadow, the lower side of human nature, and at least begin to work upon transforming the negative into something positive. Hence the importance of knowing the deeper level of significance of the year 2012. This also helps us to understand why some people write of 2012 as a kind of "stepping into paradise," because in a certain respect—at least, potentially—this is true. It also helps us understand why others write of tremendous catastrophes associated with the end date of the Maya calendar in 2012, which could also be true if humanity does not prepare to receive the great wave of Divine Love, preparation for which entails undergoing purification. Purification can be undertaken voluntarily. On the other hand, catastrophe brings with it the necessity of new orientation and, correspondingly, purification.

To summarize, the work of Christ in returning in an ethereal form in the twentieth century has been—and continues to be—to prepare humanity as a whole to receive and come into harmony with and unite with the approaching great wave of Divine Love from the Central Sun—the event described by Rudolf Steiner as World Pentecost, a galactic alignment, just as Pentecost in AD 33 was an alignment with the Central Sun at the heart of our galaxy. Rudolf Steiner's life was dedicated to preparing humanity for the awakening of Christ consciousness in order that as many human beings as possible are able to experience the World Pentecost positively. As Christ was descending from above in ethereal form to enter into the Earth's etheric aura in 1933, Rudolf Steiner was striving on an ascending path to meet with Christ descending from the cosmos.[16] In Rudolf Steiner's biography, toward the end of his life, a very significant event took place through which Christ's path of descent met with Rudolf Steiner's ascending path so that he was able to receive directly from the Etheric Christ. Through this encounter, which took place at Christmas 1923, Christ imparted to Rudolf Steiner a direct transmission (infusion) though which he was imbued with a cosmic impulse from the Etheric Christ. The nature of that impulse is best characterized by the words Divine Love. As a result of this encounter, through Rudolf Steiner the Etheric Christ gave to humanity a meditation—the Foundation Stone Meditation—in which is encapsulated that which is called the Foundation Stone of Love, and through this meditation it is possible to enter into the impulse of Divine Love which is an expression of the direct presence of the Etheric Christ in our time. This came through Rudolf Steiner for the whole of humanity and is something of extraordinary significance! Working with the Foundation Stone of Love helps one to enter into the right level of vibration to be able to receive the great wave of Divine Love that is coming at the World Pentecost.[17]

---

16   The year 1899 denotes the dawn of the New Age, the beginning of the return of Christ into the Earth's etheric aura, a process that took thirty-three and one-third years to complete, on January 8, 1933—thirty-three and one-third years being the length of Christ's life. As described below, later in this appendix, some twenty-four years into this period—on December 25, 1923—a most significant occurrence within this process took place, corresponding to the *baptism* in relation to the Etheric Christ. This baptismal event at Christmas 1923 is evident when it is cognized that Rudolf Steiner stood in relation to the Etheric Christ, preparing the way for him, in a way analogous to that of John the Baptist who prepared the way for the coming of Christ into a physical body at the baptism in the River Jordan.

17   Paul & Powell, *The Foundation Stone Meditation in the Sacred Dance of Eurythmy.*

There are many other aspects relating to the present time that are discussed in the book *Christ & the Maya Calendar*. One important aspect concerns the forces of darkness opposing the coming of Christ. Because of the approaching World Pentecost, the forces of darkness know that they do not have much time to accomplish their agenda, which is to take over the world, including humanity and the whole of nature. There are all kinds of phenomena in the present world that are working upon the consciousness of human beings in a negative way. Whereas Christ respects individual human freedom, these opposing forces do not, and they work not only upon adults, who are at least capable of freedom of choice through exercising their free will (based upon a conscious understanding of what is entailed in making a choice), but also upon children and young people in all kinds of ways.

In particular, the opposing forces work through certain aspects of modern technology. There are all kinds of ways in which a young person's consciousness is captured by modern technology. It is not unusual to find a thirteen-year-old who will come home from school and go to their bedroom, which is equipped with their own television set and computer, not to mention the omnipresent mobile phone, in the privacy of the bedroom then to enter into a virtual world, to a large extent cut off from the rest of the family. Moreover, more and more sophisticated technologies are arising to seduce the consciousness of young people, who in former times would play in nature or with friends, and who often used to have something of an inner religious life, including prayer and even meditation. It used to be natural for a child between the age of seven and fourteen to come into some form of religious consciousness—turning toward the angels or toward God. Nowadays, there is hardly a possibility of turning toward the angels, because the mobile phone is in use, or there is some other technological distraction, preventing the interior dialogue that is the foundation for suprasensory experience. How can young people receive communications from their guardian angel when they are constantly bombarded by technology? This is an enormous challenge in our time. This is not to say we should not use technology, because it is undoubtedly very useful on a practical level.

However, we have to be aware of the negative impact of technology, and how this negative impact is affecting precisely the part of us we call the life body or the etheric body through which we are able to connect with Christ!

As a remedy to this attempt by the forces of darkness to penetrate and harden our etheric bodies, endeavoring to cut us off from Christ and attempting to prevent us from being open and receptive to the gift of Divine Love, we need to strengthen our etheric body and open ourselves to the meeting with Christ, whose being is Divine Love and who is seeking, above all, to unite with human beings. However, it is important that we turn to him in freedom, and open ourselves to him whose being is unfathomable mercy. It is Rudolf Steiner's great gift to humanity to have brought into existence a new form of sacred move-ment—eurythmy—which strengthens the etheric body and prepares us for union with the being of Christ in his ethereal form at the pres-ent time, as the bearer of Divine Love and unfathomable mercy and compassion. Eurythmy is by no means the only way, yet it is one of the ways offering a path leading to what is needed as a preparation for the approaching great wave of Divine Love.

Whether or not the onset of the great wave of Divine Love signify-ing World Pentecost will be around December 21, 2012, or sometime later remains to be seen. Apart from the Maya calendar, there are other prophecies that point to this time period as a time of transi-tion.[18] In the last analysis, however, it is difficult to pinpoint with any degree of accuracy the exact time when our solar system will exit the region of cosmic dust and debris in this local part of the galaxy in which our Sun—on its path around the Central Sun—has been tra-versing now for some 5,120 years. However, that the World Pentecost will come, of this we can be sure. And it is essentially and intrinsically an inner event for which inner preparation is required.

In light of the foregoing, it emerges that Christ's incarnation some two thousand years ago is now being replicated, but on a different level. Two thousand years ago the events surrounding Christ's com-ing unfolded on the physical level in the region of Palestine, whereas now they are taking place on a global level, impacting the whole

---

18 Powell & Dann, *Christ & the Maya Calenda),* chapter 10.

world. And now the time-scale is different, extending over a much longer period of time than the 3½ years of Christ's ministry. Rudolf Steiner's Christ experience in 1899, denoting the commencement of his mission to proclaim the coming of the Etheric Christ, can be likened to the beginning of John the Baptist's mission in AD 29. The flow of the baptismal waters of Rudolf Steiner's proclamation to his followers culminated in their participation in the profound baptismal event of the Christmas Foundation Meeting—the giving of the Foundation Stone Meditation on December 25, 1923. Even the time at which the Foundation Stone Meditation was first spoken (10 AM) coincides with the time (10 AM) of the baptism of Jesus in the River Jordan on September 23, AD 29.[19] As Rudolf Steiner indicated, he heard the words of the Foundation Stone Meditation from the World Logos (Christ). Just as the Logos descended to unite with the physical vessel provided by Jesus of Nazareth at the baptism in the Jordan, so the Etheric Christ descended to unite with the vessel created by the assembled people at the Christmas Foundation Meeting and spoke to those gathered there through the words of the Foundation Stone Meditation spoken by Rudolf Steiner.

Through bringing down the Foundation Stone of Love from cosmic heights—in the shape of a dodecahedron (this being the form, visible in the etheric realm, of the "Grail stone")—the Etheric Christ began his work of preparing humanity for the World Pentecost, just as two thousand years ago Christ during the 3½ years of his ministry prepared his twelve disciples for the event of Pentecost at the galactic alignment on May 24, AD 33. What has not been described here is where the crucifixion and resurrection of the Etheric Christ fit into this discussion. This would lead too far afield, to go into right now. Instead the focus in this appendix is upon the Etheric Christ's baptismal event on December 25, 1923, paralleling the event of the baptism of Jesus in the River Jordan on September 23, AD 29, on the one hand, and upon the World Pentecost event—if the Maya prediction is correct, due to commence with the galactic alignment on December 21, 2012—paralleling the historical Pentecost event at the galactic alignment on May 24, AD 33. Whether the event of World Pentecost

---

19 Powell, *Chronicle of the Living Christ*, pp. 37–38.

will occur exactly when the galactic alignment occurs on December 21, 2012, or whether it will take place at some later point in time (for example, around 2230, when the Sun at the winter solstice will align with the galactic center), it is important that we consciously prepare for it. It is quite possible that the World Pentecost will actually be an unfolding process, starting with an initial in-streaming of the Pentecostal wave of Divine Love at the end of the Maya calendar on December 21, 2012, and gradually intensifying until the Pentecostal wave of Divine Love culminates with the alignment of the Sun at the winter solstice with the galactic center in approximately 2230.[20] To immerse oneself in the words of the Foundation Stone Meditation is a potent way of preparing oneself for the coming great wave of Divine Love signifying World Pentecost. As expressed in the closing words of the Foundation Stone Meditation, words through which the human being turns to the Etheric Christ for his light in one's mind, his love in one's heart, and his goodness in one's will:

---

20   This process would correspond to a gradual emergence of our Sun (and solar system) from the region of cosmic dust and debris left from the remnants of the Sagittarius Dwarf Galaxy's assimilation into the Milky Way Galaxy: "For only a few percent of its 240-million-year orbit around the Milky Way galaxy does our Solar System pass through the path of Sagittarius debris. Remarkably, stars from Sagittarius are now raining down onto our present position in the Milky Way. Stars from an alien galaxy are relatively near us" (professor of astronomy Steven Majewski, discussing the two-billion-year-old shape of the Sagittarius debris trail in relation to the structure of our Milky Way Galaxy, at http://blogs.discovermagazine.com/badastronomy/2007/06/27/is-the-sun-from-another-galaxy/). Regarding the date (approximately 2230) of the alignment of our Sun at the winter solstice with the center of the Milky Way Galaxy, it is interesting to note that this date coincides closely in time with the year 2234, which marks the end of the Age of Michael (1879–2234). The Age of Michael is the current archangelic period for humanity and the Earth. The archangelic periods, each 355 sidereal years in length, are a succession of historical periods in which, during each period, one of seven Archangels, in succession, assumes the task of guiding humanity and the Earth: Michael/Sun (607–152 BC); Oriphiel/Saturn (152 BC–AD 204); Anael/Venus (204–459); Zachariel/Jupiter (459–814); Raphael/Mercury (814–1169); Samael/Mars (1169–1524); Gabriel/Moon (1524–1879); and Michael/Sun (1879–2234). The period of 355 years is associated with the planet Mercury, during which Mercury completes 1,474 orbits of the Sun and, simultaneously, 1,119 synodic periods (orbits of the Earth). See Steiner, *From the History & Contents of the First Section of the Esoteric School, 1904–1914*, in which he refers to the archangelic periods, though without giving a precise dating.

O Light Divine, O Sun of Christ,
warm thou our hearts,
enlighten thou our heads,
that good may become
what from our hearts we found
and from our heads direct
with single purpose.

This is the essence of what is needed by way of preparation for the approaching World Pentecost.

A Note from the Author

Rudolf Steiner's large body of research known as *spiritual science* (Anthroposophy) has paved the way for further research encompassing thousands of volumes and numerous projects and social endeavors around the world. This book focuses on Steiner's indications about the Second Coming, the return of Christ in the etheric, on the one hand, and the incarnation of Ahriman on the other. Both events, according to Steiner, are taking place, or will take place, in our time. The author's goal in this book is to provide a context in which the reader can find help in understanding the larger picture regarding the nature of the times in which we are living. The purpose of this book, therefore, is to draw attention to Christ's return in the realm of life forces known as the *etheric* and to point out the impending physical incarnation of Ahriman (the Antichrist of Christian tradition). This book has been carefully written in the spirit of the age of the clear, critical consciousness of modern humanity so that readers may draw their own conclusions. Thus, it is not a matter of pointing the finger and pronouncing slogan-like statements. Rather, it is a matter of providing a *context* for the reader to arrive at a deeper grasp of what is taking place in the world at the present time. This can be done only through hard study and one's honest endeavor to attain a higher level of cognition. The main point is that the incarnation of Ahriman is actually the shadow side of the much greater event of Christ's coming in the etheric realm, whereby Divine Sophia is actively working to help humanity to become aware of this greatest event of our time: the Second Coming.

Central to Rudolf Steiner's impulse is the development of intuitive faculties, which he named *Imagination, Inspiration,* and *Intuition.* This means that, when research is presented, people—through the exercise of their own intuitive faculties—come to their *own* cognition of the truth and do not depend simply on what is said by those presenting the research. The goal is—and must be— to arrive at truth *for oneself* and not rely solely on someone else's statements. Nevertheless, the statements of others can be taken as a starting point for reaching the truth on one's own. Cognition of the truth depends on the development of the individual's own intuitive faculties and on going beyond intellectual speculation.

Since the publication of my earlier book *Christ & the Maya Calendar* (coauthored with Kevin Dann), various pronouncements have been made—many of a speculative nature—concerning the content of that book, and such statements may well be made also about the present book. While fully supporting the free expression of thought and the freedom of speech underlying such statements, clearly an author cannot be held responsible for conclusions drawn by others from the research presented in a book. My sole concern as an author is truth, in the spirit of these words: "You shall know the truth, and the truth shall make you free" (John 8:32).

In relation to the Antichrist of Christian tradition (the incarnated Ahriman)—referred to as the *Beast* in chapter 13 of the Book of Revelation—his way, according to Revelation 13, is prepared by the *Prophet of the Beast* (see table on page 31). Nowhere in this book are statements made that identify specific individuals as the Beast (Antichrist) or as the Prophet of the Beast. Yet, in this age of the Internet, all kinds of pronouncements can—and probably will—be made in the public domain. A responsible approach for modern human beings is to exercise caution and discretion in relation to such statements and to seek—through the development of the aforementioned intuitive faculties—to arrive at the truth for oneself, together with the One who said: "I am the way, the truth, and the life" (John 14:6).

BIBLIOGRAPHY

Andreev, Daniel. *Rosa Mira: Die Weltrose,* Frankeneck, Germany: Vega, 2009.

———. *The Rose of the World,* Great Barrington, MA: Lindisfarne Books, 1997.

Anonymous. *Meditations on the Tarot* (trans. R. Powell), New York: Putmam/Tarcher, 2002.

———. *The Mysterious Story of X7,* Berkeley, CA: North Atlantic Books, 2009.

Azuma, Ronald T. "A Survey of Augmented Reality," in *Presence: Teleoperators and Virtual Environments,* Columbus; Ohio State University, Aug. 1997.

Charles, Prince of Wales. *Harmony: A New Way of Looking at Our World.* London: Blue Door/HarperCollins, 2010.

Christian Star Calendar, ed. Robert Powell), San Rafael, CA: Sophia Foundation Press, published annually until 2009; continued as *Journal for Star Wisdom* (see below).

Dice, Mark. *Big Brother: The Orwellian Nightmare Come True,* San Diego: The Resistance, 2011.

Engdahl, F. William. *Seeds of Destruction: The Hidden Agenda of Genetic Manipulation* Montreal: Global Research, 2007.

Journal for Star Wisdom (ed. Robert Powell), Great Barrington, MA: SteinerBooks, published annually.

Koehle, Orlean. *Just Say No To Big Brother's Smart Meters: The Battle Against Smart Meters, Their Harmful, Untested RF Emissions and Other Forms of EMF—Electromagnetic Frequency Emissions,* Rohnert Park, CA: ARC, 2011.

Madsen, John. *The New Testament: A Rendering* (Edinburgh, Scotland: Floris Books, 1994.

Murdock, James. *The Syriac New Testament,* Boston: H. L. Hastings, 1896.

Mutwa, Vusamuzulu Credo. *Indaba, My Children: African Folk Tales,* New York: Grove: 1964.

O'Leary, Paul V. (ed.). *The Inner Life of the Earth: Exploring the Mysteries of Nature, Subnature, and Supranature,* Great Barrington, MA: SteinerBooks, 2008.

Paul, Lacquanna & Robert Powell, *The Foundation Stone Meditation in the Sacred Dance of Eurythmy*, Palo Alto, CA: Sophia Foundation of North America, 2007.

Powell, Robert. *The Christ Mystery: Reflections on the Second Coming*, Fair Oaks, CA: Rudolf Steiner College Press, 1999.

——. *Chronicle of the Living Christ*, Hudson, NY: Anthroposophic Press, 1996.

——. *Elijah Come Again: A Prophet for our Time: A Scientific Approach to Reincarnation*, Great Barrington, MA: Lindisfarne Books, 2009.

——. *The Morning Meditation in Eurythmy: Four Levels of Bringing to Realization "Not I but Christ in me,"* San Francisco: Sophia Foundation (study material), 2006.

——. *The Most Holy Trinosophia: And the New Revelation of the Divine Feminine*, Great Barrington, MA: SteinerBooks, 2000

Powell, Robert, and Kevin Dann. *The Astrological Revolution: Unveiling the Science of the Stars as a Science of Reincarnation and Karma*, Great Barrington, MA: SteinerBooks, 2010.

——. *Christ & the Maya Calendar: 2012 & the Coming of the Antichrist*, Great Barrington, MA: SteinerBooks, 2009.

Sebag Montefiore, Simon. *Stalin: The Court of the Red Tsar*, New York: Random House, 2003.

——. *Young Stalin*, London: Orion, 2007.

Solovyov, Vladimir. *War, Progress, and the End of History: Three Conversations, Including a Short Tale of the Antichrist*, Hudson, NY: Lindisfarne Press, 1990.

Steiner, Rudolf. *The Bhagavad Gita and the West: The Esoteric Meaning of the Bhagavad Gita and its Relation to the Letters of St. Paul*, Great Barrington, MA: SteinerBooks, 2009.

——. *The Book of Revelation: And the Work of the Priest* (CW 346), London: Rudolf Steiner Press, 2008.

——. *The Festivals and Their Meaning*, London: Rudolf Steiner Press, 2002.

——. *Freemasonry and Ritual Work: The Misraim Service: Texts and Documents from the Cognitive-Ritual Section of the Esoteric School 1904–1919* (CW 265) Great Barrington, MA: SteinerBooks, 2007.

——. *From the History & Contents of the First Section of the Esoteric School 1904-1914* (CW 264) Great Barrington, MA: SteinerBooks, 2010.

———. *The Incarnation of Ahriman: The Embodiment of Evil on Earth* (CW 254), London: Rudolf Steiner Press, 2006.

———. *Karmic Relationships: Esoteric Studies*, vol. 4 (CW 238), London: Rudolf Steiner Press, 1956.

———. *The Occult Movement in the Nineteenth Century*, London: Rudolf Steiner Press, 1973.

———. *An Outline of Esoteric Science* (CW 13), Hudson, NY: Anthroposophic Press, 1997.

———. *The Reappearance of Christ in the Etheric*, Great Barrington, MA: SteinerBooks, 2003.

———. *Spiritual Guidance of the Individual and Humanity: Some Results of Spiritual-Scientific Research into Human History and Development*, Hudson, NY: Anthroposophic Press, 1992.

———. *The Sun Mystery and the Mystery of Death and Resurrection: Exoteric and Esoteric Christianity* (CW 211), Great Barrington, MA: SteinerBooks, 2006.

Starlight Newsletter (Sophia Foundation of North America), online at http://sophiafoundation.org/newsletter/ (semiannual).

Sucher, Willi. The article "In Memory of Willi Sucher (1902–1985)," originally published in the *Journal for Star Wisdom 2010*, has been edited and made available as "Willi Sucher and Jeane Dixon's Prophecy" at: www.steinerbooks.org/detail.html?id=9781584201113.

Tomberg, Valentin. *Inner Development*, Hudson, NY: Anthroposophic Press, 1992.

Von Halle, Judith. And If He Had Not Been Raised…: *The Stations of Christ's Path to Spirit Man*, London: Temple Lodge Press, 2007.

———. *Descent into the Depths of the Earth on the Anthroposophic Path of Schooling*, London: Temple Lodge, 2011.

———. *Vom Leben in der Zeitenwende* (Life at the Turning Point of Time), Dornach, Switzerland: Verlag für Anthroposophie, 2009.

Warnke, Ulrich. *Bees, Birds and Mankind: Destroying Nature by "Electrosmog": Effects of Wireless Communications Technologies*, a Brochure Series by the Competence Initiative for the Protection of Humanity, Environment and Democracy.

Zelikovsky, Victor. *2012: Prophecies of the Emerging Golden Age*, Oberwil, Switzerland: Metaphysica Publications, 2008.

✝

COMPUTER PROGRAM: Peter Treadgold, *Astrofire* (distributed by the Sophia Foundation of North America, Palo Alto, California). *Astrofire* has a comprehensive research module for data storage and comparison charts, a star catalog with over 4,000 stars, and a database of birth and death charts of historical personalities. It is capable of printing out geocentric and heliocentric/hermetic sidereal charts and ephemerides throughout history. With this program one can compute birth charts in a large variety of systems (tropical, sidereal, geocentric, heliocentric, hermetic); calculate conception charts using the hermetic rule, in turn applying it for correction of the birth time produce charts for the period between conception and birth; print out an "astrological biography" for the whole of life with the geocentric and heliocentric planetary systems; work with the sidereal zodiac according to the definition of your choice (Babylonian sidereal, Indian sidereal, unequal-division astronomical, etc.); work with planetary aspects with orbs of your choice. Included are eight house systems and a variety of chart formats. It includes an ephemeris program with a search capability. *Astrofire* runs under Microsoft Windows. If you are interested in *Astrofire,* please contact:

> Sophia Foundation of North America
> 525 Gough St, #103
> San Francisco, CA 94102
> Phone/fax: 415-522-1150
> sophia@sophiafoundation.org
> www.sophiafoundation.org

Astrofire can be purchased online from the Sophia Foundation website:
sophiafoundation.org/astrosophy/astrofire/

CHRIST & THE MAYA CALENDAR
2012 & THE COMING OF THE ANTICHRIST

ROBERT POWELL AND KEVIN DANN

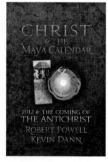

Despite the explosion of books, videos and TV shows that claim to penetrate the mystery of "2012"—the numerical shorthand for the completion on December 21, 2012, of the thirteenth B'ak'tun cycle in the Long Count of the Maya calendar—consensus about its meaning seems to remain elusive. The discussion about the significance of 2012 falls generally into two distinct camps: "New Age" authors who see this date as marking the advent of an imminent, universally accelerated psychic/spiritual evolution and professional astronomers and ethnologists who generally discount such metaphysical claims

Christ and the Maya Calendar approaches the significance of 2012 by spiritually penetrating phenomena of today. Drawing on the book of Revelation—which provides an archetype for understanding spiritual history, as well as Rudolf Steiner's Apocalyptic indications—a completely new context for grasping the end date of the Maya calendar emerges.

In addition to penetrating the spiritual background of our time in relation to the coming of the Antichrist (the incarnation of Ahriman), the authors explore the significance of the Mexican mysteries and present a wealth of new research with the intention of helping the reader to navigate the Apocalyptic scenario currently shaping up, with the global financial crisis as one important expression. Most important, the authors refer to the Second Coming of Christ as the true event of our time, with the incarnation of Satan/Ahriman as its shadow. The authors also show the significance of Divine Sophia as the antidote to negative consequences of Ahriman's incarnation.

www.steinerbooks.org | ISBN: 9781584200710 | 280 pages | paperback | $25.00

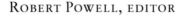

JOURNAL FOR STAR WISDOM

ROBERT POWELL, EDITOR

The *Journal for Star Wisdom 2012* is a special edition that addresses directly the challenges facing humanity in our time. It includes articles of interest on star wisdom (Astrosophy), as well as a guide to the correspondences between stellar configurations during the life of Christ and those of today. This guide comprises a complete sidereal ephemeris of geocentric and heliocentric planetary positions and an aspectarian for each day through the year. Published yearly, new editions are available beginning in October or November for the coming new year.

According to Rudolf Steiner, every step taken by Christ during his ministry between the baptism in the Jordan and the resurrection was in harmony with—and an expression of—the cosmos. The *Journal for Star Wisdom* is concerned with the heavenly correspondences during the life of Christ and is intended to help provide a foundation for Cosmic Christianity—the cosmic dimension that has been absent from mainstream Christianity in its two-thousand-year history.

Readers are invited to contemplate the current movements of the Sun, Moon, and planets against the background of the zodiacal constellations (sidereal signs) in relation to corresponding stellar events during the life of Christ. In this way, it becomes possible to open oneself to attune to the life of Christ in the etheric cosmos.

The main focus of this year's journal is the significant year of 2012 as a pivotal year in the history of humanity and the Earth.

Journal for Star Wisdom 2011

www.steinerbooks.org | ISBN: 9780880107280 | 154 pages | paperback | $25.00

Journal for Star Wisdom 2012 available November, 2011

ISBN: 9780880106528 | special expanded edition | $30.00

THE CLOCKWISE HOUSE SYSTEM
A TRUE FOUNDATION FOR SIDEREAL AND TROPICAL ASTROLOGY

JACQUES DORSAN

Jacques Dorsan was the leading pioneer of sidereal astrology in France. Using more than eighty sidereal horoscopes, this book illustrates Dorsan's clockwise house system. Most of the charts are from the original French edition, with many more added in this edition. The book embodies one of the most important astrological discoveries of twentieth and twenty-first centuries. Astrology normally views the twelve houses in astrology in a counterclockwise direction, the direction of the zodiac signs. According to Jacques Dorsan, however, we should view them in a clockwise direction.

Traditionally, Western astrologers have interpreted the houses as though they rotate in the same, counterclockwise direction as the zodiac signs. According to Jacques Dorsan, however, the houses are enumerated in a clockwise direction, following the daily diurnal motion of the Sun, for example. By using the clockwise house system together with the sidereal zodiac, everything suddenly falls into place astrologically when looking at a horoscope. This key unlocks the mystery of the horoscope. Thanks to Jacques Dorsan, we finally have access to a true form of astrology—based on the sidereal zodiac and utilizing the clockwise house system—enabling a giant leap forward in the practice of astrology. It allows us to recover the original astrology. This is possible today because of Rudolf Steiner's indications, as well as the research of the French statistician Michel Gauquelin, who investigated hundreds of thousands of horoscopes and confirmed that the astrological houses run in a clockwise direction.

This English translation includes more than eighty charts, both those in the Jacques Dorsan's original work in French and more added by the editor of this edition. The clockwise house system is applied in this book using sidereal horoscopes. It can just as easily be applied using tropical horoscopes.

www.steinerbooks.org I ISBN: 9781584200956 I 330 pages I paperback I $30.00

Elijah Come Again
A Prophet for Our Time
A Scientific Approach to Reincarnation

Robert Powell

The research presented by Robert Powell in this book shows that a new science of the stars is possible, based on a study of reincarnation and karma. Willi Sucher did much to pioneer the development of a new star wisdom, or astrosophy, as a scientific tool for the investigation of karma. Powell has discovered that applying the science of astrosophy to the findings of karma research reveals—through the discovery of astrological reincarnation rules—the foundations underlying star wisdom. Once these foundational findings relating to astrological reincarnation research have been assimilated, a reformation of traditional astrology will inevitably take place. Once the new astrology is established, there will be a similar feeling in looking back upon traditional Western astrology that modern astronomers have when looking back upon the old geocentric astronomy.

The purpose of *Elijah Come Again* is to contemplate the incarnations of the prophet Elijah, with the goal of laying the foundation for a new "science of the stars" as the "science of karma." At the close of his last lecture, after discussing the sequence of incarnations of Elijah–John the Baptist-Raphael–Novalis, Rudolf Steiner spoke of this individuality as "a radiant and splendid forerunner...with whom you are to prepare the work that shall be accomplished at the end of the [twentieth] century, and will lead humankind past the great crisis in which it is involved." These words indicate that, from the end of the twentieth century and into the twenty-first century (that is, now), the Elijah–John individuality is to be a "radiant forerunner" for humanity in the next step underlying our spiritual evolution.

Elijah Come Again presents a scientific approach toward unveiling the mystery of human destiny.

www.steinerbooks.org I ISBN: 9781584200703 I 260 pages I paperback I $35.00

THE ASTROLOGICAL REVOLUTION
UNVEILING THE SCIENCE OF THE STARS
AS A SCIENCE OF REINCARNATION AND KARMA

ROBERT POWELL AND KEVIN DANN

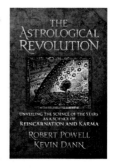

The basis of Western astrology, the tropical zodiac, emerged through Greek astronomers from what was originally a calendar dividing the year into twelve solar months. The fact that ninety-eight percent of Western astrologers use the tropical zodiac means that contemporary Western astrology is based on a calendar system that does not reflect the actual location of the planets against the background of the starry heavens. In other words, most astrologers in the West are practicing a form of astrology that no longer embodies the reality of the stars.

Drawing on specific biographical examples, *The Astrological Revolution* reveals new understandings of how the starry heavens work into human destiny. For instance, the book demonstrates the newly discovered rules of astrological reincarnation through the previous incarnations of composer Franz Schubert and his patron Joseph von Spaun—respectively, the Sultan of Morocco, Abu Yusuf Ya'qub, and his erstwhile enemy, Alfonso X, the Castilian King known as "El Sabio" (the Learned), along with their sidereal horoscopes. Rudolf Steiner's biography is also considered in relation to the sidereal zodiac and the rules of astrological reincarnation.

After reestablishing the sidereal zodiac as a basis for astrology that penetrates the mystery of the stars' relationship to human destiny, the reader is invited to discover the astrological significance of the totality of the vast sphere of stars surrounding the Earth. *The Astrological Revolution* points to the astrological significance of the entire celestial sphere, including all the stars and constellations beyond the twelve zodiacal signs. This discovery is revealed by studying the megastars, the most luminous stars of our galaxy, illustrating how megastars show up in an extraordinary way in Christ's healing miracles by aligning with the Sun at the time of those miraculous events. *The Astrological Revolution* thus offers a spiritual—yet scientific—path of building a new relationship to the stars.

www.steinerbooks.org | ISBN: 9781584200833 | 254 pages | paperback | $25.00

ASTROSOPHY

The Sophia Foundation of North America was founded and exists to help usher in the new Age of Sophia and the corresponding Sophianic culture, the Rose of the World, prophesied by Daniel Andreev and other spiritual teachers. Part of the work of the Sophia Foundation is the cultivation of a new star wisdom, *Astro-Sophia* (Astrosophy), now arising in our time in response to the descent of Sophia, who is the bearer of Divine Wisdom, just as Christ (the Logos, or the Lamb) is the bearer of Divine Love. Like the star wisdom of antiquity, Astrosophy is sidereal, which means "of the stars." Astrosophy, inspired by Divine Sophia, descending from stellar heights, directs our consciousness toward the glory and majesty of the starry heavens, to encompass the entire celestial sphere of our cosmos and, beyond this, to the galactic realm—the realm that Daniel Andreev referred to as "the heights of our universe"—from which Sophia is descending on her path of approach into our cosmos. Sophia draws our attention not only to the star mysteries of the heights, but also to the cosmic mysteries connected with Christ's deeds of redemption wrought two thousand years ago. To penetrate these mysteries is the purpose of the yearly *Journal for Star Wisdom.*

For information about
Astrosophy/Choreocosmos/Cosmic Dance workshops
contact the Sophia Foundation of North America:
525 Gough St. #103, San Francisco, CA 94102
(415) 522-1150; sophia@sophiafoundation.org;
www.sophiafoundation.org

ROBERT POWELL, Ph.D., is an internationally known lecturer, author, eurythmist, and movement therapist. He is founder of the Choreocosmos School of Cosmic and Sacred Dance, and cofounder of the Sophia Foundation of North America. He received his doctorate for his thesis *The History of the Zodiac* (available as a book from Sophia Academic Press). His published works include *The Sophia Teachings*, a six-tape series (Sounds True Recordings), as well as the books shown on these pages and in the bibliography. He is also the author of *Christian Hermetic Astrology; The Christ Mystery; The Sign of the Son of Man in the Heavens;* and other works published by Sophia Foundation Press (sophiafoundation.org). He translated the spiritual classic *Meditations on the Tarot* and translated (with James Morgante) Valentin Tomberg's *Lazarus, Come Forth!* Robert teaches a gentle form of healing movement: the sacred dance of eurythmy (from the Greek, meaning "harmonious movement"), as well as the cosmic dances of the planets and signs of the zodiac, and through the Sophia Grail Circle, he facilitates sacred celebrations dedicated to the Divine Feminine. Robert offers workshops in Europe, Australia, and North America and, with Karen Rivers, cofounder of the Sophia Foundation, leads pilgrimages to various sacred sites of the world: 1996, Turkey; 1997, the Holy Land; 1998, France; 2000, Britain; 2002, Italy; 2004, Greece; 2006, Egypt; 2008, India; 2010, Grand Canyon; and South Africa, 2012. Visit sophiafoundation.org.

Lightning Source UK Ltd.
Milton Keynes UK
UKOW050621170911

178831UK00003B/12/P